THE HYENA
SCIENTIST

THE HYENA SCIENTIST

text by *Sy Montgomery*   photographs by *Nic Bishop*

HOUGHTON MIFFLIN HARCOURT
Boston   New York

For Dr. Millmoss and Mr. Thurber —S. M.
For Africa —N. B.

CONTENTS

AFRICA

MOROCCO

ALGERIA LIBYA

EGYPT

MAURITANIA MALI NIGER

SUDAN

CHAD

NIGERIA

SOUTH
SUDAN

ETHIOPIA

KENYA SOMALIA

EQUATOR

D.R.
CONGO

TANZANIA

ANGOLA

ZAMBIA

NAMIBIA ZIMBABWE

BOTSWANA

SOUTH
AFRICA

KENYA

Lake
Turkana

EQUATOR

• Nairobi

MASAI
MARA

• Malindi
• Mombasa

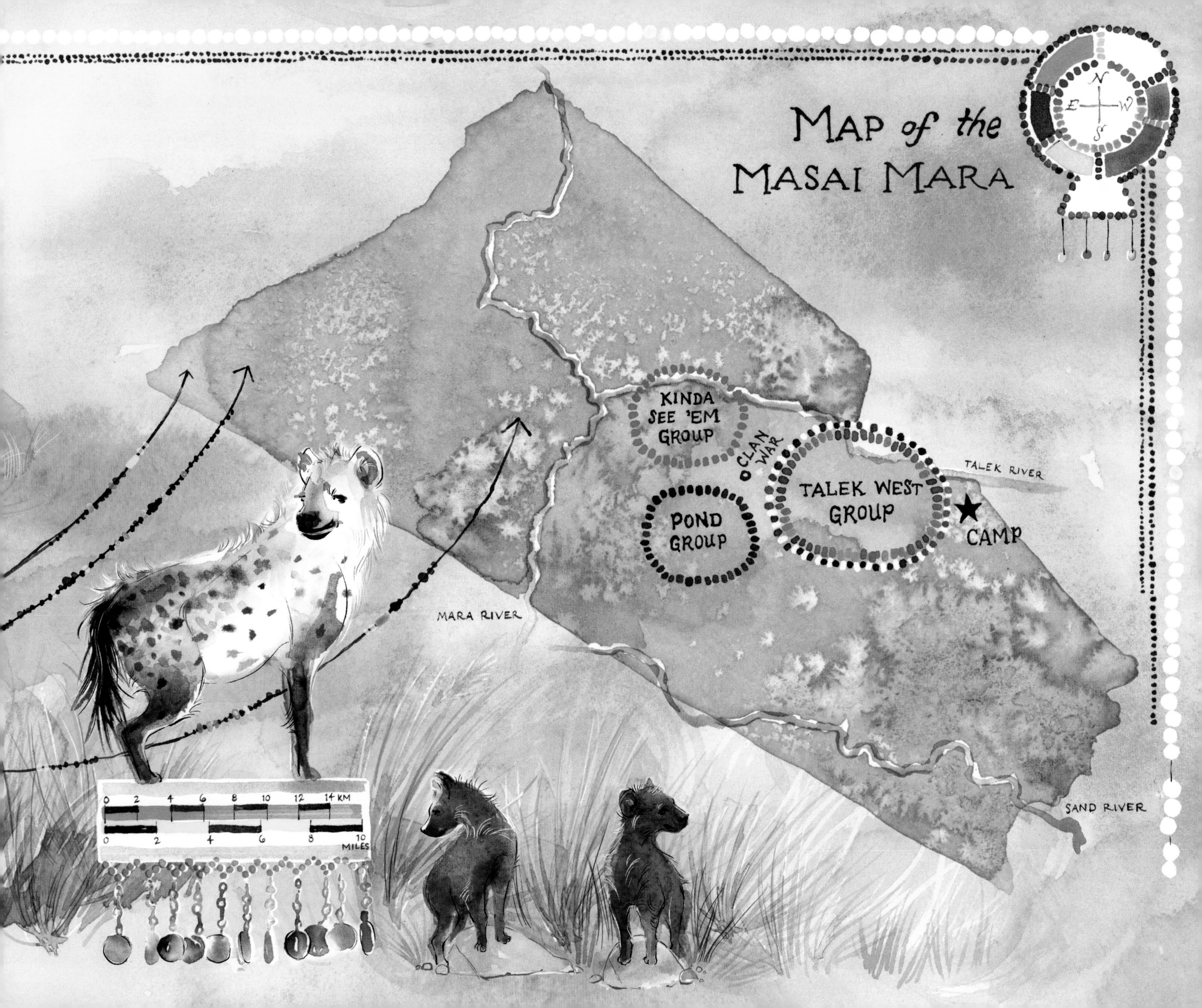

MAP of the
MASAI MARA

KINDA
SEE 'EM
GROUP

CLAN
WAR

TALEK WEST
GROUP

TALEK RIVER

POND
GROUP

★
CAMP

MARA RIVER

SAND RIVER

0 2 4 6 8 10 12 14 KM

0 2 4 6 8 10
MILES

Hyena society is built on strong social bonds.

CHAPTER ONE

A Most Misunderstood Mammal

At the den, the fluffy, spotted babies play like puppies, dashing and lunging, wrestling and spinning. Tiny infants, still coal black and lacking their spots, sit on opposite sides of a patient, older cub—each chewing gently on an ear of their tolerant sibling. Nearby, an even younger infant nurses contentedly from his mother, who's sacked out on her side. She lifts her head, tilting her tall, expressive ears forward, and looks through the windshield of our Land Cruiser into our faces. There is no malice in her wide, brown eyes, just innocent interest. Reassured it's only us, the mother lays her head back down and relaxes with her baby.

With long, dark muzzles, blond coats with black spots, bristly black tails, and ears that look like a cross between a teddy bear's and an elf's, these animals could easily be mistaken for some exotic breed of dog. But they are only distant relatives of man's best friend—and far more distant in human affection. Their species is almost universally despised across human cultures. Feared for biting children, hated for digging up corpses, dismissed as cowardly scavengers, the loving, social, attractive animals playing and resting in front of us are widely considered to be dirty, ugly, and mean.

They're not the monsters people fear. Nor are they what they seem. Though they look like dogs, they separated from the ancestors that would lead to the dog lineage some fifty million years ago, back when Antarctica was still lined with tropical rainforests. They are actually more closely related to cats, and even more closely related to mongooses. But they don't really belong with the mongoose tribe, either: they belong to their own family, the Hyenidae, a group that includes only four species: the little-known aardwolf—a small, striped termite-eater—and the striped hyena, the brown hyena, and the species before us, the spotted hyena.

Modern hyenas, like humans, are a recent evolutionary invention, perhaps less than one million years old. Our two lineages grew up together. In fact, at least one biologist has suggested that hyenas are the reason so few fossils of early humankind exist in Africa: hyenas, whose strong jaws can crush bones and whose tough guts can digest them, ate the skeletons of our ancestors. Bad PR goes back a long time in our relationship.

"Hyenas inspire horror in people," wrote wildlife biologist Hans Kruuk. "Hyenas are inexorably linked with garbage cans, corpses, feces, bad smells, and hideous cackles."

In *Green Hills of Africa*, Ernest Hemingway called the hyena a "devourer of the dead, trailer of calving cows, ham-stringer, potential biter-off of your face at night while you slept, sad yowler, camp-follower, stinking, foul, with jaws that crack the bones the lion leaves, belly dragging, loping away on the brown plain . . ."

A century before he penned those words, Samuel Griswold Goodrich noted in his *Illustrated Natural History of the Animal Kingdom* that, while archvillains like Aaron Burr and Judas Iscariot had their defenders, it seemed no one would say a kind word about hyenas. Even Disney's movie *The Lion King* managed to portray hyenas as conniving, cowardly thieves.

Just yards from our vehicle, the fuzzy cubs scamper around the den, bucking and twirling, as the golden light of an African afternoon haloes the plush fur on their ears. "How can you *not* like hyenas when you see *this*?" asks Kay Holekamp, sixty-four, a zoologist from Michigan State University. "They're adorable!" Kay's behind the wheel of our Land Cruiser here in southwest Kenya's Masai Mara, one of the most spectacular wildlife reserves in Africa, and she knows each of these cubs by name—as well as their mothers, fathers, grandmothers, and in many cases, great-grandmothers.

The spotted hyena is Africa's second largest carnivore, after the lion.

Kay's research on the spotted hyena is one of the longest continuously running field studies of any mammal in the world. Kay has been at it for three decades—and her findings are clearing up the animal's bad rep, revealing the spotted hyena as an unexpectedly brave, smart, and extremely social species.

Instead of a skulking scavenger, the spotted hyena is a skilled and mighty hunter. It's the second biggest, and the most formidable, carnivore in Africa—yes, Kay tells us, even more formidable than the lion. Though all hyenas but aardwolves evolved from scavenging ancestors, and they will happily devour any food they can find, Kay has found that spotted hyenas (unlike the striped and brown) directly kill 60 to 95 percent of the food they eat. A single 130-pound female is capable of

Hyenas are formidable carnivores. These have brought down a topi.

running down and killing, unaided, a bull wildebeest three times her own weight—and can consume thirty pounds of meat (the equivalent of 120 quarter-pound hamburgers!) in half an hour.

Spotted hyenas are keystone predators who control the health of the ecosystem. "Take hyenas out of the picture and all kind of things would go out of control," says Kay. That once happened in South Africa, when farmers decimated hyenas and their fellow predators. The result? Ecological disaster: explosions of herbivores reduced grasslands to deserts. Soil erosion ruined roads and altered the course of rivers. Only when the predators returned did the ecosystem begin to recover.

Kay has pioneered a new way of looking at hyenas, showing them in an entirely new light. "Hyenas are often pictured slinking around, hassling the 'real' predators—waiting to steal food from a lion," Kay notes. "But very often, it's the other way around." As it turns out, lions steal food from hyenas more often than hyenas steal from lions.

Instead of a filthy, smelly brute, the spotted hyena is a creature who spends a considerable amount of time and effort on grooming. "Sure, they have bad hair days," admits Kay—hyenas sometimes lie in mud to cool

Newborn cubs have dark fur, which gets lighter as they age.

off in the African heat. "But then they groom themselves and become spiffy clean." Because their tongues are rough like cats' tongues, hyenas can use them like fine-toothed combs on their fur. They groom both themselves and each other. Mothers are particularly attentive to their babies' hygiene, going so far as to clean under their cubs' tails when necessary.

Even the hyena's fabled laugh isn't what people think. There's nothing funny about it to a hyena. Instead of a hysterical giggle, it's actually a sound of excitement, or even fear, uttered, for instance, when someone—like a lion—attacks the hyena or steals its food. And the giggle is just one of the astounding sounds in the hyena's extensive vocabulary: They rumble (typically a sign of worry). They groan (usually a mother calling her cub). They low like contented cattle (when hyenas are preparing for a coordinated behavior, like mobbing a rival group). Their impressively rich repertoire ranges from the elastic *whoop*s that echo through the African night—sometimes to announce the presence of a kill, sometimes to gather fellow hyenas for a group activity, and sometimes a complete mystery—to the cubs' high-pitched *eeeeee!,* known as squittering, which babies use to demand "more milk!" from their moms.

In a way, it's no wonder that people get

hyenas so wrong. "Hyenas are like no other animal," Kay says. "They're the coolest animals out there, because they are just really weird."

For starters: hyena females look like males. In most mammals, the males are bigger than the females. With hyenas, not so—the females are 10 percent bigger. And if you check underneath, both males and females look alike. It's so confusing that years ago, when a collector was sent to capture hyenas for a zoo, he reported he could find only males . . . until, that is, one of his captured "males" gave birth in front of his eyes—though a tube-like organ

that looked exactly like male equipment. ("It's like giving birth through a soda straw!" comments one of Kay's assistants.) For years, people believed hyenas were hermaphrodites, each with both male and female sex organs. Today scientists know that's not true, but they're still awed—and perplexed—by the evolutionary forces that sculpted such a bizarre female reproductive tract.

Among hyenas, sex roles are reversed. Females are far more aggressive. Ladies rule in hyena society—a very rare situation among mammals. And hyena society is unusually

A cub makes a squittering call when begging for milk.

Wildebeests are a favorite prey animal for spotted hyenas.

rich and complex, composed of clans that can number more than one hundred individuals. All members of the clan know each other, and each has an assigned rank, inherited from birth, which everyone in the clan knows and respects. Though each individual hyena may spend much time alone or in small groups, clan members cooperate to raise cubs in communal dens. They defend a common territory from rival clans. In this way, hyena society is sort of like a feudal kingdom—except the kings are queens.

"Hyenas appear to violate the rules of mammalian biology," says Kay. That's what makes them so fascinating and important to study. "Studying the oddballs can teach you about the basics," Kay explains. They allow us to gain insight into what the rules actually are.

"Spotted hyenas can teach us a tremendous amount about a lot of different things," Kay insists. Over her many years of study, she has hosted more than one hundred grad students and research assistants, each pursuing some different aspect of hyenas' mysteries. How did their social networks and intelligence evolve? How do sex hormones affect aggression and dominance? What do hyena vocalizations mean? What roles do postures, gestures, and scent marking play in communication?

The questions go on and on. And solving mysteries about hyenas may have unexpected applications. For instance, notes Kay, "Their immune systems are amazing; they can eat anthrax and survive. Wouldn't it be great if hyenas could give us a way to help people recover from food poisoning?"

Then, there are their teeth: hyenas' teeth are the only ones in the animal kingdom strong enough to crack the massive leg bones of a giraffe. "Car companies want a synthetic paint as strong as the enamel on hyena's teeth!" Kay says. "And . . ."

She could continue, but a newcomer arrives at the den. She's a radio-collared female, and Kay doesn't even have to swing her binoculars up to her eyes to identify who this is: "It's BUAR!" she announces—which is the four-letter code for her real name, Buenos Aires. She's the highest ranking female, the leader of the group, the undisputed queen of the clan. "Hi, BUAR!" Kay greets the seven-year-old matriarch like an old friend. Which she is.

Kay has followed BUAR's life ever since she was born in December of 2009. She has measured every part of her body, examined her blood and feces, tracked her movements, followed her children. After BUAR's mother, Murphy, was killed by a lion in April 2011,

Kay and her students chronicled BUAR's rise to the throne, to the top of the hyena hierarchy.

To meet BUAR and the clan she rules, photographer Nic Bishop and I have come to Kay's camp here in Masai Mara. We'll accompany Kay and her research team as they study the Talek West Clan—one of several hyena clans in the area. BUAR's is the mightiest of the empires. Talek West is the largest hyena clan ever recorded, with 130 animals—three times larger than most estimates of average clan size elsewhere.

Last summer, Kay tells us, her research team began seeing evidence of a possible split in the clan. If such an event is really happening, it will pit sisters against sisters, mothers against daughters—a drama worthy of Shakespearian tragedies or Hollywood action films. We're hoping to catch a glimpse into hyena society at what might be a critical turning point in the Talek West Clan's history. It's a rare opportunity to add a fascinating piece to the puzzle of understanding hyenas' rich and complex social system.

Nic and I could watch the babies play at the den forever, but it's time to check on what other members of the clan are doing. "Let's back off," says Kay, "and see what else we can find."

KAY'S STORY

Kay always loved animals. But growing up in a suburb of Saint Louis with her younger brothers and sister, their dogs, cats, and rabbits (along with wild snakes and turtles they caught and freed), she had no idea how far that love would take her.

When she was fifteen, Kay was accepted for an internship at the Saint Louis Zoo. Her boss, Dee White, was the head of the Children's Zoo, at a time the institution was constructing a new nursery for baby animals. Curly-haired, fun-loving, and just a few years older than Kay, Dee introduced her to exotic and appealing animals: binturongs, big civets from Southeast Asia with thick, furry, grasping tails, and kinkajous, night-loving, rainforest tree-dwellers who stuck their long tongues into people's ears. "I thought I'd be happy working in a zoo," said Kay.

At Smith College in Massachusetts, Kay studied captive mouse possums, little South American marsupials. She completed a catalog of all their different behaviors, the first ever compiled. After graduating, she landed a job as a tour guide in Colombia, near the Brazilian border. She hoped to see her mouse possums in the wild.

There Kay found a world shockingly different from the university lab or the zoo.

One of the first people she saw upon arrival in Colombia was grabbing insects out of the air and eating them. Another woman she met showed her a scary tropical fungus that had developed on her leg. And in the room next to Kay's, a parrot mimicked the sound of a crying baby, screaming all night. "I thought maybe I should catch the next plane home," Kay remembers. "But in three days, I realized: I'm going to like this place!"

While in Colombia, she met the man she would later marry, a PhD candidate in economics who loved exploring as much as she did. They set out to travel the world together. Back in the States, both paused their academic studies to work painting houses to raise money for their trip. A year later, they stuffed all their belongings into a day pack and arrived in East Africa.

Kay saw hyenas for the first time in Ngorongoro Crater, part of the Serengeti ecosystem, in Tanzania. Camping without a tent, she and her husband were woken one night by a hyena who had come to investigate them in their sleeping bags. Not long after, they watched a pack of hyenas run down and kill a wildebeest.

"They're not just skulking carrion eaters," Kay realized. She was intrigued.

After Tanzania, the couple took a boat across the Indian Ocean to India, hitchhiked to Nepal, hiked in the Himalayas, and visited Burma, Thailand, Malaysia, and Indonesia before moving back to the States. Both earned PhDs. Kay pursued a study of American ground squirrels. She and her husband amicably divorced.

Kay never forgot the hyenas. While she was working as a postdoc at University of California, Santa Cruz, a former advisor was working with a colony of captive hyenas. He was intrigued that, unlike most mammalian societies, the females were not subordinate to the males. "Wouldn't it be interesting to go into nature and understand what happens in the wild?" he suggested to Kay one day over lunch. "I thought you'd be a good person for this."

With a grant to fund her early research, Kay visited carnivore biologist Laurence Frank at his research site in Masai Mara; he had been studying hyenas since 1979, but was soon to return to the States to concentrate on studies of a captive colony. Many members of the colony were hyenas he had captured just outside the park and raised from cubhood. Laurence deeply admired the hyenas, and the hand-raised animals at the US colony snuggled with him affectionately. But Kay noticed the wild hyenas fled at the approach of his car. No wonder: when he shot them with tranquilizer darts, the gun

Kay catches up on email in her tent at Fisi Camp.

produced two loud explosions, which scared everyone. The animals who witnessed the darting were terrified, and the darted animals woke up with bloody notches in their ears, which Laurence had cut to help him identify individuals. She decided to do things differently.

Her study began on May 15, 1988. Working with longtime friend Laura Smale, a neuroscientist at Stony Brook University, Kay vowed to do nothing, ever, to hurt or frighten the hyenas. She would stop notching their ears and instead learn the hyenas' identities by memorizing their spots.

She would find a quieter dart gun, and never fire it near other hyenas. And for the first two years of the study, she and Laura kept their distance. They visited the den, respectfully and quietly, every day. "If the animals looked uncomfortable, we backed off," she said. Then, they gradually got closer. The animals soon learned to recognize their car as harmless and allowed the researchers to approach closely.

The hyenas learned to recognize not only the women's car but their faces, too. Once, Laurence Frank returned to his old study site in Kay's vehicle. The hyenas, remembering the dartings, saw his face through the windshield—and fled.

This was yet another sign of hyenas' extraordinary social intelligence—and another intriguing feature of the species. "Originally we were thinking of a three-year project," Kay remembers. "But the hyenas were so bizarre and so interesting it gave rise to a whole set of new questions." Are there different kinds of intelligence? How does intelligence itself arise? How do females dominate males in this complex society? How do individuals learn their rank? What happens when young males leave their families? Does their rank at birth still affect them?

When she began, Kay's study included only fifty hyenas. The closest town, Talek, had only a few hundred people, with no school or hospital. (When local Masai needed medical care, they went to Kay, who they called "Mama Fisi"—Hyena Lady. She'd fix them up as best she could, or stop her work to drive them to the hospital in Narok.) Because few people hassled them, the hyenas didn't need to choose dens concealed by thick brush, so Kay and Laura got glorious views.

Things have changed in the nearly thirty years since Kay and Laura began their study. Laura returned to the States to resume her neuroscience studies. Kay joined the Michigan State University faculty in 1992, where both women now work; the two married in 2016. Now Kay's students run her hyena project most of the year, and she joins them in the summer. More than one hundred students have spent more than a year in Masai Mara. For most of them, it's a "life-changing experience," she says. Students especially appreciate learning from the Masai, who "are happy without endless material possessions."

Over the eight generations of hyenas Kay has studied, the Talek West Clan has grown to 130 animals; her students are now researching the lives of four other clans, the Fig Tree Clan and three clans near a second camp, called Serena, as well. From just three tents, her research site has grown to include two separate, well-equipped

camps, each two hours' drive apart. The town of Talek has grown tenfold, to perhaps as many as eight thousand residents. Even though it's against the law, because it endangers wild animals, Masai increasingly graze their cattle, sheep, and goats in the Masai Mara reserve. The hyenas have adapted; they increasingly scavenge garbage around the nearest human settlements. They nab the occasional cow, sheep, or goat that grazes unaccompanied in the reserve. And now the hyenas usually choose dens hidden at least in part by dense brush.

Kay's groundbreaking studies have helped revamp people's understanding of one of Africa's top predators. She and her students have published more than 150 scientific papers. Her work has been honored by the American Society of Mammalogists, the American Association for the Advancement of Science, and the American Academy of Arts and Sciences. "There are literally no other studies like hers," says her colleague Dorothy Cheney, a University of Pennsylvania professor who studies baboons in Botswana. "She has the patience and fortitude to persevere"—despite African bugs, snakes, heat, sickness, floods, funding issues, political instability, and study subjects who can be both shy and aggressive.

Even after all these years, the hyenas remain fascinating. No matter how many questions she's able to answer with her studies, Kay says, "they just keep getting more interesting."

In a quiet moment at camp, Kay and Dee play cribbage on a board Dee drilled into a hippo bone.

CHAPTER TWO

Fisi Camp

"Welcome to Fisi Camp!" When we arrive after eight long, hot, dusty hours on the road from Nairobi, the busy, congested capital of Kenya, Kay welcomes Nic and me to the small, tented community in the bush that will be our Kenyan home away from home. Fisi (pronounced "FEE-see") means hyena in Swahili, the most common language in East Africa, and the name of this camp is an apt one, since sometimes the study subjects come right into camp, along with a variety of other animals. We're eager to meet them.

We're thrilled to have finally reached our destination. On our way from Nairobi, we passed businesses with intriguing names: the Mongoose Property Cares real estate company; the Mamba Shop, selling Cokes instead of the deadly serpent for which the store was named; the Rhino Cement company, whose product boasted great strength; and the improbably named Blessings Butcher Shop—surely no blessing for the animals who supplied its merchandise. Our Land Cruiser shared the Great North Road, a paved highway built by Italian POWs in 1942, with cars, trucks, overcrowded minibuses called *matatus*, bikes, and donkeys. One bicyclist ferried a full-size couch, balanced precariously on the cycle's seat.

Then, about ninety miles later, at the town of Narok, the smooth paving of the Great Road abruptly gave out. "The road ahead is not very good," our driver, Lawi Maruka, told us. "It's bumpy. So prepare for an 'African massage'!"

We bumped and rattled over the rutted clay road, past deep-green bushes drooping with poisonous white datura blossoms, past red-flowering flame trees and umbrella-shaped, thorny acacias. Roadside poinsettias grew to the size of saplings, flanked by banana plants, maize gardens, and herds of belling

Sitting in the dining tent are, from left,
Ciara, Jared, Amy, Dee, and Kay.

cows with their herdsmen. Many of the men and women we saw draped their shoulders with red-checkered shawls called *shukas*. Beaded earrings, bracelets, and necklaces sparkled against their skin. Most of the people, Lawi explained, were Masai—the tribe of tall, brave, cattle-owning people after whom the Masai Mara Game Reserve is named. (*Mara* means "mottled," a reference to the patchy landscape of grassland and scrub.) As we neared the gate to the reserve, we spotted wildebeests, zebras, gazelles, ostrich, and African crowned cranes—birds whose heads seem adorned with spiky gold hairdos.

Now that we've arrived at last, Kay introduces us to the people who will be our companions for the next ten days:

DIANA "DEE" WHITE, 69. She hired Kay more than forty years ago, when Kay was fifteen and Dee was working as a zookeeper at the Saint Louis Zoo. Now retired from a career as a medical social worker, Dee serves as Kay's data manager and assistant.

CIARA MAIN, 24. "Everyone thinks I'm Kenyan, until I open my mouth," she says. Though she speaks quite a bit of Swahili, her American accent gives her away. Ciara began her stint as a research assistant last June, skip-

African crowned crane.

ping her graduation ceremony from University of California, Davis, to instead attend a research conference in Alaska before leaving for Kenya days later.

JARED GRIMMER, 23.
He arrived the same month as Ciara, from Kalamazoo College, in Michigan, where he majored in biology and became engrossed with animal behavior. With a feather tattoo celebrating his Native American heritage (his dad is Chippewa) on the inside of one arm, he has loved animals and the outdoors since he was a kid, and he is especially interested in exploring the individuality of each creature.

AMY FONTAINE, 23.
After graduating with a degree in wildlife biology from Humboldt State University, in California, Amy next studied wolves and coyotes in Yellowstone National Park. She's the newest research assistant, having been in camp less than two months.

BENSON OLE PION, 25.
A Masai herdsman with a wife, two children, and a herd of cattle, goats, and sheep, Benson started working at Fisi Camp as an assistant cook. But hyenas captured his imagination, and as his interest in them grew, so did his knowledge. Kay hired him as a research assistant in 2011.

Kay's KENYAN SUPPORT STAFF also contributes importantly to the success of Fisi Camp. Joseph Ole Kamaamia, assisted by Samwell Ole Kamaamia and Chief Ole Pion, cooks breakfast and dinner ("Ole" means "son of" in the Masai language, Maa). Two Masai *askaris*, or guards, Steven Ole Karkar and Lusingo Ole Naurori, patrol camp at night. Brandishing their spears, they evict animals who might pose a nuisance or a danger—which happens remarkably often since the camp is not fenced.

"Baboons and vervet monkeys invade, and pee and poop everywhere," explains Dee, "especially in the kitchen."

"There could also be lions," adds Jared. Once the staff found nine of them lounging in the camp's parking area.

"And always watch for snakes," warns Ciara.

"I stepped over a baby cobra on my way to the shower," notes Dee.

As our new friends escort Nic and me along the dirt path to our tents—large, comfortable nine-by-fifteen-foot canvas rooms big enough for a bed, desk, and chair, and tall enough to stand in—Jared points out an essential accessory to each tent's front fly: the confluence of the three zippers has been stuffed with a sock. This feature was added after Jared returned from the field one day

Chief washes dishes.

Joseph (left) and Samwell (right) make pancakes.

A sock helps keep out snakes.

The choo takes a little getting used to.

Fisi Camp is tucked under the shelter of trees.

to discover a black mamba intently trying to squeeze through the small opening between the zippers to gain entry. Widely considered the most deadly snake in Africa, the snake was so feared that the Masai staff not only killed it, but then burned its corpse.

Next on the tour is the shower. Screened by several green tarps wrapped around trees and open to the sky, it's an ingenious Rube Goldberg contraption whose operation requires several steps:

1. Upon approach, call out *"hodi, hodi!"* (pronounced "HOH-dee, HOH-dee") so as not to surprise a fellow researcher in a state of undress.

2. Remove ant-proof lid from large plastic rain barrel and place solar-powered pump inside.

3. Reach finger up inside hanging plastic housing for solar-powered electric switch. First, though, note wasp nest inside housing and check whether wasps are in residence.

4. Discover matches inside plastic bag beneath bucket and remove to light kerosene heater. To do this, first unhook metal latch and swing small fuel reservoir open, checking to see it has a wick. If not, get dressed again and fetch one from the kitchen.

5. After lighting, ignore sound like jet aircraft landing, calmly swing reservoir back, and close latch.

6. Turn on cold and

7. hot faucets. Test temperature to make sure water isn't scalding.

Turning it all off is an equally elaborate affair. But well worth it for a hot shower after a long, sweaty day in the African heat.

Our next stop, down a path and beneath an acacia draped with a discreet vine, is the *choo* (pronounced "choh"). Again, before entering, one must call *"hodi, hodi!"* to

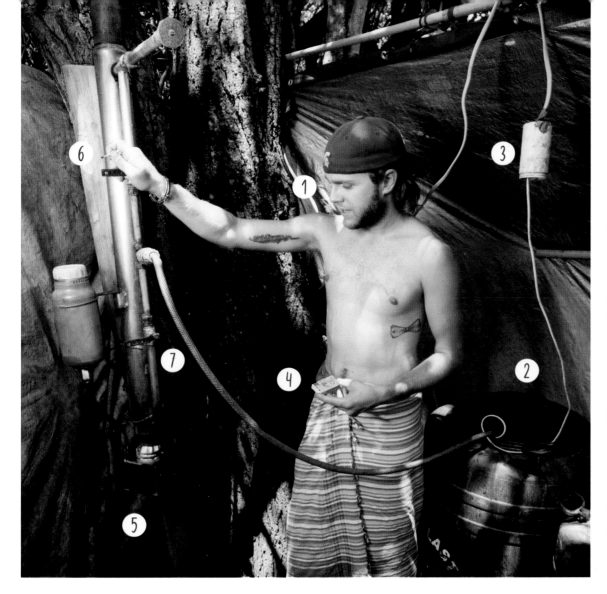

tree and fitted with a spigot serves as a hand-washing station.

Nic and I adjourn to our tents to unpack, and then we join the rest of the team in the twenty-by-fourteen-foot research tent that also serves as a dining room. As we enjoy Joseph's meal of roasted chicken, stuffed mushrooms, and rice, bats join us for dinner, swooping overhead to eat the moths who gather around the solar-powered light at the tent's ceiling.

As night falls, the dark throbs with unseen voices: fruit bats beeping like electric alarm clocks, nightjars whistling like lonely ghosts, jackals calling with rusty-hinge squeaks. Insects and frogs chime, tick, pop, hum. Two nights ago, in their tents up the hill, Kay and Dee were kept awake by the deep, grunting roars of two amorous hippos. Dee could easily translate the conversation: "'I LOVE you! I LOVE you!' We were like, 'get a room!'"

But it's not till I'm snug in my bed that I hear the nighttime welcome I've been waiting for: the haunting *ooooOOO-WHOOP!* of a distant hyena, calling to her family in the night. And then, from another direction, comes the answer: *ooooOOOO-WHOOP! ooooOOOO-WHOOP!* Back and forth they go, their voices swinging to and fro like a cradle, an African lullaby that melts into my dreams.

ensure privacy. Walled, like the shower, in green canvas, and open to the sky, the toilet is a wooden seat atop a sturdy wooden box, perched above a deep hole. Jared shows us how, by using one foot to wiggle a flat stone placed strategically in front of the seat, you can coax many of the insects out of the hole. When he demonstrates the technique, to our amazement, an impressive cloud of about a hundred flies and a dozen bees rises from the pit and flies out of the toilet. "The bees are stingless," he assures us cheerfully. "And there's a pair of flycatchers"—handsome, long-tailed birds—"who love to hang out here and eat the flies. We named them Pee Wee and Marjorie." A pink plastic bucket tied to a

DEE'S STORY

Few women worked as zookeepers back in the 1960s. Dee was one of them. And shortly after the Saint Louis Zoo completed its Children's Zoo and animal nursery, she accepted Kay as a high school volunteer there. "She was fantastic—an animal fanatic with an innate sense of what to do," Dee remembers. "And now I work for her. It's come full circle."

But the circle took a long time to come around.

Dee loved the zoo and the animals there. She planned to become a veterinarian. She dreamed of one day going to Africa, to see many of the animals she knew from the zoo in the wild. But over the next forty years, it seemed her hopes and dreams were dashed, one by one.

At the zoo, when Dee wanted to work with adult animals, male zookeepers threatened to quit if the management promoted her. A woman couldn't do the job, they said. (Today, most zookeepers are women!) In college, Dee enrolled in the preveterinary classes—one of two women among two hundred men on the animal husbandry track. She was discouraged at every turn. The professors—all male—"thought women were a waste of time and space," she remembers. Dee left school, met a man she loved, and they got engaged. He was drafted, and was killed in the Vietnam War.

Dee went back to college and studied medical social work. She took a job as a genetic social worker, helping people to make decisions about their lives based on the revelations of DNA testing. She still loved animals. She still longed to visit Africa and see the wild creatures there. "Africa was my dream," she says, "but it seemed like a dream deferred—and then a dream lost."

Forty years after the Saint Louis Zoo built its animal nursery, the zoo invited Dee to a reunion. "I was thinking about Kay," she says, "so I Googled her name." She was overwhelmed

Dee at work in her tent, recording the day's data.

with information about this internationally acclaimed woman researcher conducting one of the longest and most important studies of African mammals in the history of science. Dee sent Kay a message: "Are you the same Kay who I hired in high school?" Fifteen minutes later came the reply. "I can't believe it's you. You inspired me. You have to come to Africa!"

Dee took much of her life savings and bought a ticket to Africa to meet Kay there and visit her study site. "I had a massive anxiety attack before my plane even reached Atlanta," she admits. But once there, the two friends reconnected. Kay hired Dee as her assistant during the summers, and as a data manager for the hyena study the rest of the year. At age sixty-nine, Dee's dreams have all come true.

"I'd like kids to know," says Dee, "don't ever give up on something you care about. You never know what's going to happen!"

Tent repair is just one of many camp chores.

Kay scans the landscape for hyenas. The antenna on the roof is used to radio-track animals.

CHAPTER THREE

Morning Obs

In the predawn dark, we gather in the research tent at five fifteen a.m. to down quick cups of tea, load the car with binoculars, telemetry gear, and the thick notebook of all the hyenas' photos, and fill our water bottles before departure. While Jared stays in camp to type up his field notes, Kay, Ciara, Nic, and I will leave in one Land Cruiser, and Amy, Dee, and Benson will take another. It's our first time on "obs"—short for observations— which happen each morning and evening, weather permitting. In the cool of the early morning, hyenas, like most sensible animals in Africa, are more active. Kay starts up the car and heads west. "Let's see if we can find something!" she says.

"I'm going to start tracking," Ciara announces. She tunes in a receiver mounted to the dash, trying to pick up signals from any of the dozen radio-collared hyenas in the study who might be nearby.

"Good morning," Ciara narrates into the mike for the digital voice recorder. "Today is May 16, time 5:35. Observers are Ciara, Kay, and two guests." Researchers and assistants record observations of hyenas and other carnivores, as well as time and place the animals

Inside the vehicle, GPS gives location data while the receiver can scan for individual hyenas.

were seen, with Global Positioning System coordinates. The info will later be transcribed and inputted to the study's massive database to reveal the patterns: who hangs out with whom, who outranks whom, what times and routes are busiest, how hyenas interact with each other, and how they react to other carnivores.

"At 5:38, we see Decimeter, wandering south," Ciara says. "We are two hundred thirty meters northwest of Croton Island, GPS 0749764 East, 9837532 North . . ." Kay's and Ciara's sharp eyes can just make out three-year-old Decimeter, a daughter of Queen BUAR. "And I'm picking up Helios," adds Ciara into the mike. Though we can't see

Helios in the tall grass, the radio signal confirms her identity: each collared hyena has his or her own "channel," and Helios's frequency is 151.170 megahertz. The signal's strength indicates she's within fifty yards of us. Ten years old, Helios is the second-ranking female in the clan.

One minute later, Decimeter meets up with another hyena. Kay recognizes this hyena immediately from his spot pattern. It's Decimeter's younger brother, year-old Kilometer—both were named after units of measure. They greet each other with a hyena salute: each raises a back leg so the other can sniff the undercarriage, inhaling the sibling's familiar, unique perfume. They both head west, along with Helios, whom we can now see. "You're basically seeing one big family here," says Kay.

Ciara takes sounds recordings of the hyenas.

This radio-collared hyena is named Hendrix.

We try to follow them along the muddy, rutted track, but they disappear into the tall grass.

"5:44. We have a lion . . . two lions," Ciara narrates into the mike. The huge, maned, tawny cats to the right of the track are probably brothers—and may be a problem. "Lions kill more hyenas than anything else but people," Kay tells us. "We just worry about them . . ." A pair of black-backed jackals trots through the grass. These small, doglike carnivores may be hoping for scraps from a nearby impala carcass, Kay observes.

"5:49: Bora is seen," Ciara notes. "And that's . . . Shrimp in the back. That's Amazon's cub. And Picometer, walking west . . . Here's Buenos Aires again, and following her is a cub . . . no, two cubs, following by eighty meters: Joule, the larger, and littermate Kilo . . ."

"Everybody's heading home," says Kay. While the researchers go out each morning and evening, in the dark of night the hyenas are too difficult for Kay's crew to see. But Kay knows the action doesn't stop when the researchers aren't watching. "They must have had a night of some excitement, with all those lions and jackals! The den is right ahead of us, in this thicket."

Black-backed jackal.

HYENA BEHAVIOR IN SHORTHAND

Hyena scientists use a sort of shorthand to record different behaviors they observe in the field. (The complete catalog of all an animal's behaviors is called an ethogram.) Here's a sampling:

BRT: Bristletail. Tail is lifted and bristled like a bottlebrush, indicating excitement, including but not limited to aggression.

EBBO: Ears back, back off: a lower-ranking hyena, feeling threatened by a dominant one, signals submission by flattening the ears backwards against the top of the head and backing off.

T-1, T-2, T-3: Threat levels for aggressive behaviors. T-1 is the mildest. T-3 is a serious threat and usually results in a bite.

OMA: Open-mouth appease. One animal puts his or her open mouth up to another's. It's a gesture meant to dispel any aggression before it actually happens.

DP: Defensive parry. Similar to OMA, but in response to actual aggression. A threatened animal uses his or her mouth like a catcher's mitt to protect itself against bites, since hyena jaws and teeth are so imposing and strong.

LL: Lift leg. A way to initiate a greeting, like a salute or extending a hand to shake. Usually two hyenas stand head to tail and each raises a leg to make it easier for the other hyena to sniff his or her undercarriage.

APP/AV: Approach/avoid. One animal approaches another, stops, looks submissive, and backs off, but still remains facing the animal of interest. Usually adult males do this when they feel conflicted about approaching a sexy female. Females are always dominant, so males have to watch their step.

ST OV: Stand over. One animal stands with head high and muzzle pointed down at shoulders of a second individual. This behavior reminds the other animal who's dominant.

MOB: Mobbing. Two or more hyenas bunch up as a group to approach a threat, like a lion or rival hyenas, in an attempt to drive them away.

HB: Head bob. Wagging the head up and down or sideways as a sign of submission. Tiny cubs instinctively bob their heads at everyone, including plants waving in the wind—until they learn their rank among the who's who of the clan.

This hyena is doing an open-mouth appease because he is subordinate to the smaller pups.

The communal den, made of usurped and enlarged tunnels originally dug by warthogs, jackals, or aardvarks, may offer as many as twenty different entrances. With its deepest tunnels too tight for anyone but cubs to squeeze through, it offers a safe, cool place for babies to hide below, and an area for family to gather and meet above. Kay discovered that a hyena group moves to a new den every few months, when ticks or fleas prove bothersome—or worse, if a lion visits.

This site is known as Dave's Den, named by the grad student who first found it. Though the den is surrounded by a thicket, when Kay positions the car, we get a great view of the hyenas interacting with one another, and an unrivaled opportunity to document the hyena hierarchy.

"What's absolutely critical to know is who's who," Kay explains. Though her predecessor on the project, University of California researcher Laurence Frank, used to cut notches into the hyenas' ears to help him tell them apart, Kay discovered she could identify each individual by their spot patterns. She developed a sort of hyena yearbook, with photos of both the left and right sides of each hyena, which every researcher tries to memorize and consults in case of doubt.

Ciara now recognizes another mom at the den, nine-year-old Amazon, by the butterfly-shaped spot on her left side. Twister, another mom, has a unique spot that looks to Ciara like a ghost. Cub Urc (short for Urchin, in a litter named after sea creatures) has a swirl like a cinnamon roll on his left side, while sibling POW (short for Portuguese Man of War) has spots forming three lines parallel to his body.

A bit easier, but equally crucial, is learning to recognize what the hyenas are actually doing. A lunge is different from a parry, and an open-mouth appeasement is different from a yawn. Even a stare—which is different from a look—has meaning in hyena society, as well as the position of the ears (laid back against the head when backing away in deference to a dominant animal, or cocked forward when attacking a lower-ranked animal), tail (up and bristling in excitement, tucked in retreat), and mouth (an open mouth may indicate submission or threat). All, Kay has found, are important in hyenas' complex communication system.

She's still trying to nail down exactly what each vocalization and each posture and gesture means. To help her, Kay had a life-size robot hyena built at Michigan State University, with a camera in its face and a speaker in its mouth. The robot could raise and lower its head, move its ears, and raise, lower, and bristle its tail. It

At the den, a piece of jawbone becomes a toy to play with.

was built to be tested at a captive hyena colony in California, to see how hyenas responded to each signal. But the funding for the colony ran out in 2009 and the hyenas recently went to new homes. Unfortunately the robot is too heavy to ship to Africa, so until another US-based hyena colony appears, Kay says ruefully, "It's a sculpture in my lab," keeping her company over the long, hyena-less months before she returns to Kenya each summer.

But the live hyenas before us are providing plenty of action to document right now. Cubs are playing and mock-fighting, springing and chasing, leaping like little acrobats. Another cub chews on a bone. While the parents don't usually bring food to the den, sometimes they carry home horns, hooves, or tails for the babies to play with as toys. A black infant nurses from her mother, Twister. A one-year-old lays down scent from a gland beneath the tail, an activity called "pasting," which is a way of marking the clan's territory.

More hyenas arrive and greet each other, lifting rear legs so the others can sniff. Ciara attempts to narrate it all into the mike, using abbreviations to speed the story: "Amazon bristletails onto Pisces, T-1 point. Pisces E-B-B-O. [See sidebar to decode the abbreviations.] Knot emerges from bushes and pastes. Fitz whoops spontaneously." With nine hyenas in view at once, "There's too much going on!" Ciara cries. "What a great morning!" agrees Kay.

Now a new hyena appears from the west. Kay recognizes Gaza, an adult male who was born elsewhere and immigrated to Talek West. Most, but not all, young male hyenas leave the community where they're born and take up residence in a new place, a strategy that avoids inbreeding. Among the twenty adult males who've immigrated to Talek West, Gaza is very high ranking—the third from the top. And what happens next as this large, powerful male approaches the den is almost unheard of in mammalian society.

Three young cubs, Urc, POW, and Fitz, approach the big male, tails up and bristling. Big, grown-up Gaza bobs his head at them.

This is an appeasement gesture, like a soldier's salute to an officer, or a peasant kneeling before nobility. The cubs get closer and walk parallel to the big male. In response, Gaza jumps to the side, slams back his ears, backs off—and trots away.

"These cubs chased off an adult male eight to ten times their size!" Kay says. She's seen cubs boss grown-up males many times before, but she's still in awe. "Little teeny babies can dominate adult males." Urc and POW are nephews of high-ranking Helios—and as such, by birthright, they outrank any male. But also, simply because all females outrank all males, and because all babies are under their mother's care, *any* baby outranks any adult male. "It's the weirdest society in the world!" says Kay.

Biologically, what drives this odd, rigidly regimented, female-dominated society? What role, if any, do natural body chemicals like hormones play? How do the hormone levels of male hyenas differ from females, and how do high-ranking females' hormones compare with those of low-ranking ones?

Shortly after we move on from the den, we spot a low-ranking female, Baez, who offers us a piece of the puzzle that may help answer these questions: she poops.

"Great!" cries Kay, who reacts as if Baez has just offered her a treasure. In a way, she has: poop offers an easy way for scientists to see what prey species the hyenas have eaten, discover any parasites that infest their guts, and measure concentrations of many of the hormones that drive or reflect behavior. So every time a hyena poops and a researcher sees it, one of the team leaps out of the car (once the hyena has left, and making sure no other hyenas, or lions, are around) to collect it in a plastic bag for later study.

With bristled tails, the three cubs chase off Gaza, a large subordinate male.

Cubs playing at Lucky Leopard Den.

Hyenas sometimes kill cattle, which causes conflict with the Masai herdsmen.

Kay has gleaned important data from poop, including the finding that adult males' concentration of testosterone is higher in immigrant males and lower in males who don't leave their mothers' group. Ciara grabs a plastic bag and, turning it inside out, scoops up Baez's discarded treasure and labels the bag with its GPS location, Baez's name, and the time.

We drive on. We're heading farther west now, to the Lucky Leopard Den—so named because the student who found it also saw his first leopard that same lucky morning. This is the gathering place for the second of Talek West's three main social groups, sometimes called the Pond Group. Here we find another charming group of cubs. Two four-month-olds toddle and jump, mouthing each other. Two older cubs wrestle and tumble. "They're so puppy-like. No wonder people think

they're dogs," Kay says to us, as Ciara narrates into the mike.

But then, at 8:39, everyone dashes down into a hole. Soon we understand why. They hear the bells of approaching Masai cattle. A grad student from France once tested to see if hyenas could tell the difference between cathedral bells and Masai cattle bells. They could. They ignored the church bells—but the cattle bells clearly scared them. For these warn the hyenas about the approach of their worst enemies: the people who are escorting these cattle.

Because hyenas may kill goats, sheep, and cows, Kay explains, Masai will sometimes spear them—even if the hyenas are not near their livestock. They also sometimes leave poisoned carcasses to lure predators as retaliation when a predator kills any of their animals—even when it happens inside the park, where it's illegal to pasture cattle.

Two years ago, such an event killed off many of the Talek West Clan's highest rank-

ing females. All but one of their cubs starved to death as a result. Kay and her crew watched helplessly; as researchers, they couldn't step in and alter hyena history.

As if in sympathy with this sad story, dark clouds gather overhead. By the time our Land Cruiser makes it back to camp, rain is hissing down.

It should be the tail end of the rainy season by now, but May has been unusually wet this year. Global climate change makes the seasons unpredictable, and on top of that, this is a year of El Niño, a weather event that occurs every two to seven years and usually makes things even wetter. Who knows how long the rain will continue?

"This is a lot of rain, guys," says Kay disappointedly. All that water will make the ground too soft for research vehicles to leave the park's relatively few tourist tracks, which we need to do if we're to follow the hyenas. "We won't go out tonight or tomorrow," Kay says.

CIARA'S STORY

Ciara was already interested in hyenas in high school.

Hyenas? people would ask. *Really? Aren't they mean and ugly?*

But Ciara didn't care what other people thought. "I was an oddball," she admits. The adopted only child of a single white woman, Ciara credits her mom with helping her learn the discipline, courage, and respect for animals that helped her follow her dream.

Even when she was little, some of her favorite playmates while she was growing up in California were animals. Along with the family's ten rats, four dogs, and a parrot, she also loved wild animals. While other girls wanted to play with dolls, she played with wild lizards. And if the other girls didn't want to join her, that was fine with Ciara.

In elementary school, Ciara took guitar, dance, and karate lessons. By high school, she was a second-degree black belt as well as a straight-A student. Because she loved all animals, she thought she'd like to be a vet.

The summer after her sophomore year at University of California, Davis, Ciara volunteered at a center that took in unwanted animals, many of them discarded animal actors from Hollywood: chimps, a leopard, tigers, iguanas, and parrots. It was there Ciara met her first spotted hyena. Her name was Kasine.

"Don't go near the hyena," she was told. "It's dangerous."

But of course she couldn't resist. She stood and watched Kasine every day. Impressed by Ciara's patience, one worker took her aside. "C'mon, let me show you something." The worker darted to and fro. The hyena followed and started giggling. Kasine, the dangerous hyena, put her face up to the cage as playfully as a dog.

Ciara started to cry. "I was in awe of this creature, and wanted to know more."

She cried because she felt sorry for Kasine—a social animal in solitary confinement. But she also cried because she'd had a revelation.

Ciara was one of very few black students at UC Davis—the college was only 3 percent African American, she said, and the dropout rate was very high. Ciara worked hard during her college career, not only studying for the prevet track, but also volunteering, helping her fellow black students succeed. But Ciara was confused. How would *she* succeed? Did she really want to be a vet? As she stood watching Kasine in her pen, she said, "In that moment, I knew I wanted to work with hyenas, and learn what they are made of. It solidified what I wanted to do: instead of taking care of animals, I wanted to study them to learn why they do what they do."

She applied for, and won, a prestigious McNair scholarship, designed to prepare underrepresented students for graduate studies.

Looking into hyena studies, Ciara discovered "all sources lead to Kay Holekamp." She applied for, and won, a position as field assistant. "This has been my dream for a very, very long time," says Ciara.

The next step? Graduate school, where she plans to conduct her own studies of hyenas' female-dominated societies.

Ciara always keeps binoculars at the ready—both to spot distant hyenas and other predators, and to record subtle details of behavior.

CHAPTER FOUR

Maji Mingi

Like all of us, Kay is disappointed we'll have to forego a day—possibly more—of observation. But she has another reason to worry about the rain. She's thinking about the catastrophic flood of June 13.

Over dinner, Kay and Dee tell us about the event that nearly destroyed Fisi Camp the year before.

It happened at sundown. It hadn't been raining in camp, but because it had rained heavily upstream, the Talek River, which runs beside camp, had been rising all day. Normally the river is everyone's friend; camp was built by the river because it provides shade and water for essential showers and washing. But when monstrous trees came bashing down the river, Kay became alarmed.

Askari Steven assured Kay that the staff had a system to predict whether the river would overflow. "First, the water reaches this stick," he said, "and then this other stick . . ." But before he had finished his sentence, askari Lusingo came running, crying, *"Maji mingi!"* ("Much water!")

In seconds, the muddy, brown river jumped its banks. Almost instantly, the kitchen and lab tents were inundated. Wading in chest-deep, filthy water, Kay and Dee desperately ferried expensive lab equipment, like the centrifuge and the blood and fecal samples in their liquid nitrogen tanks, to higher ground, carrying the heavy objects over their heads. Floating desks, stoves, tents, file cabinets, and knives careened past them like projectiles—and the water could have brought poisonous snakes, crocodiles, and even hippos, too! But Kay, Dee, and three grad students continued to rescue the camp's most valuable equipment and data into the

night. The Kenyan staff did, too—even as everything the men owned was swept from their tents by the floodwaters. The water did not begin to recede until eleven p.m.

The next day, everything that remained was thickly coated with slimy river mud. Almost all their food was gone. Their library of valuable reference books was ruined. Almost all the tents and camp furniture were destroyed. A new Land Cruiser was submerged. For weeks afterward, they'd find medicines, chess pieces, Band-Aids, pots, knives, and beds caught in bushes around camp, ruined. Dee found a jar of peanut butter in a tree.

"We wondered if we could ever recover from that," Kay admits. For years, she has operated two camps studying hyenas—the other, Serena Camp, two hours' drive away, concentrates on three different hyena communities. But this camp—the one devoted to the Talek West Clan, the largest hyena clan ever studied—might have been finished by the flood.

Kay's grad students "worked like crazy" on cleanup for weeks, she tells us. They set up crowdfunding to replace lost gear, food, and clothing. Soon Jared and Ciara arrived, full of energy. "We were tired and beaten up," remembers Dee, "and they lifted us up."

Today, Talek West's Fisi Camp has a flood plan in place: two large tents stand staked to higher ground, ready to receive kitchen, research, and personal items in case of a flood. The spot isn't ideal, though—there's a trail nearby that might entice robbers to enter the camp. But the fear of flooding remains with Dee and Kay. For the next few days they will carefully watch the rain gauge and the river.

It rains all night. For the next two days, off-track travel to the hyenas would be impossible. But even with no formal obs, there's plenty to do in camp. Amy and Jared take inventory. Ciara transcribes the previous day's obs. Kay and Dee catch up on emails. Nic and I go with Lawi on the tourist tracks to look for wildlife. Though we stay on the least muddy tracks, we still manage to get the car stuck in mud holes twice.

The next day is market day in the town of Talek, and Amy, Ciara, Jared, Lawi, Nic, and I go in for food and supplies: potatoes, cabbages, bananas, pineapples, eggs, avocados, onions, squash, tomatoes, melons. Superglue, kerosene, scouring pads, salt shakers, airtime for cell phones. The highlight of the trip

Getting stuck is a frequent hazard of the rainy season.

Amy (left) and Jared (right) replenish food supplies on Talek's market day.

A tame eland looks for treats from the shopkeepers.

is watching a young female eland casually stroll inside the Maton Yok General Shop. The elegant, seven-hundred-pound antelope minces inside on shiny black hooves, walks right up to the counter, and accepts a treat of rice from the shopkeeper. Then she turns and leaves the building, as nonchalantly as any other satisfied shopper. We learn she had probably been adopted as an orphan and raised as a calf by one of the Masai herding families.

When we return from town, the ground is still too sodden to drive off-track and follow hyenas. But while the others return to camp

chores and recording data, Nic and I again venture out to look for animals. Right next to the track, we come upon a nursing mother hyena and her two cubs. It's an intimate, lovely family scene, the mother grooming her offspring, the babies rolling playfully on their backs, smiling like happy puppies. "What beautiful faces they have!" Lawi says in amazement. And then, as the early evening songs of frogs rise, their melodies popping like boiling bubbles, the hyena family moves off, heading to the den. A huge pink sunset with purple clouds spreads across the sky like waves on the sea.

One area of sky, bruised deep purple, holds rain. We had hoped to resume morning obs the next day. "Go away!" Amy tells the rain as it pours down on our tent through our dinner of chapatis and lentils. But it only rains harder, with thunder and lightning, and soon it's clear there will be no morning obs. In fact, it will be quite a while before any of us can even return to our tents without getting soaked.

We're all tired and eager to go to bed, but Kay and Dee are nervous. They're watching the rain gauge: Thirty millimeters. Forty. Forty-five.

Towering rain clouds have been gathering all afternoon.

At nine thirty p.m., Benson arrives from the kitchen tent where he had been eating with the staff, his Masai friends. "Fifty millimeters," he announces. "Start packing."

Ciara runs through the rain to the kitchen tent and returns back with her report. "At this moment, only the kitchen is in danger." The men are moving all the food, the stove and the storage bins to one of the two tents already erected on higher ground. But we can't afford to wait any longer. We need to begin moving the data and valuables *now*.

"Steven, go tell Lawi," instructs Kay. We will need to load his car, too, with valuables to take to higher ground.

"Want to save books?" asks Amy.

"Books and meds," answers Kay.

Amy starts stuffing the library books into waterproof river bags. Ciara packs the medicines.

Kay disappears into the storm, but soon returns, dripping. "It's coming up pretty fast," she says. I dash to my tent to get my tall boots and raincoat, to be ready for a long, wet night.

I return to find a rapid deployment force in action.

"Do we want to leave the dry boards up?" asks Jared. The dry boards list camp protocols, emergency numbers, and deadline dates.

"No," answers Kay. We remove them and pack them in Lawi's car.

"I grabbed everybody's phones," says Amy.

"All cushions in KBY," says Kay—referring to the license plate on one of her two vehicles.

Like safari ants, we move forward and carry almost everything in our path away. The liquid nitrogen tanks with their priceless samples. The computer. The centrifuge. The photo ID books. The two vortex machines for mixing samples in test tubes.

"These are the blood samples. Store them in the front seat," Dee says to me.

At ten thirty, Samwell announces the rain gauge now reads seventy-eight millimeters. The water's edge, normally fifty meters away from the kitchen, is now only half a meter away, he says. The river could overflow any minute. "It can go up two and a half meters in an hour," says Kay. A meter is 3.2 feet. You do the math.

Now, everything that can be moved from the research tent is packed in one of the three cars, except for the dining room table and chairs. We can drive to higher ground if need be. "We'll just sit here and hope for the best," says Kay.

"The water is still coming high," says Benson. "It has rained eighty-two millimeters. I have never seen eighty-two millimeters!" Not even on June 13, when the river jumped its banks—that was due to rain far upstream. But what is going on upstream from us now?

That, as much as the rain over our heads, will determine the future of Fisi Camp.

Just then, we hear the distinctive honking wheeze of a hippo. The seven-thousand-pound animal sounds uncomfortably close. The hippo is considered the most dangerous animal in Africa, because it will attack people both in the water and on land; with a mouth that can open 150 degrees wide, and twelve-inch-long canines that can weigh six pounds each, it can bite you in half. Kay and Dee's tents, if they ever get to sleep in them, lie on the other side of the hippo.

Oh, great.

"To think I thought we'd already HAD our adventure!" I say—referring to our car getting stuck in the mud, earlier in the day. That now seems a long time ago.

"You came to write about why we should all love studying hyenas," says Kay, laughing. "I hope people will still want to now!"

At 11:10, Lusingo appears and speaks to Kay in Swahili: *"Maji anaenda"*—the water is going away. *"Hakuna shida"*—no problem!

"Now it's just a matter of taking all the stuff back out, letting it dry, and putting it all back again," says Kay. It's a big undertaking for the next morning—a morning we all thought would be, if anything, *too* leisurely.

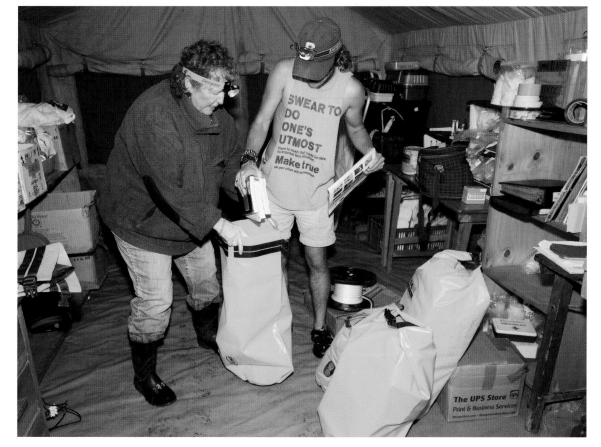

Essential items are stored in waterproof bags.

Everything is packed into the vehicles.

"But at least this time, we won't have to rewire the place," says Dee.

"Thank you, guys," Kay tells everyone. "You were great!" The askaris, bearing spears, are waiting to escort her and Dee through the half foot of water now standing between their tents, on the opposite side of the research tent from ours, and past any hippos. The rest of our group disperses to go to sleep. We're all sopping wet and cold, but camp and the precious data are safe.

I'm too keyed up to sleep at first. Lying in bed, beside the thin canvas wall of my tent, around midnight I hear heavy breathing—loud enough to be heard over the pounding rain. It's right next to my head. A large animal

The hippo is one of Africa's most feared animals.

is nearby. Somehow the sound of its breathing is comforting, reminding me of the much softer breath of my husband and border collie who would be sleeping next to me in my bed at home. Finally, I drift off to sleep.

When I wake in the morning, I notice my tent is markedly askew. It lists to the right, the corner nearest my bed collapsing. At breakfast, the askaris tell me who was there beside me last night: a mother hippo and her baby.

JARED'S STORY

Growing up in suburban Michigan with his brothers, Jared loved playing in ditches, climbing trees, and after every rain, digging up night crawlers. He loved animals—not only his family's cats, but also the creatures he'd meet outdoors, like garter snakes and toads. And he loved science. But he never thought of doing field biology for a career: "I thought, you're interested in science, you're going to be a doctor," he says, giving his usual million-dollar smile and winning, quick laugh.

So, at Kalamazoo College, Jared started down the premed track. But three special teachers changed his course.

One of them, Anne Engh, had been a graduate student of Kay's. Another was Ann Fraser, an expert on ants. And the third, Sara Tanis, also studied insects. These professors reignited his passion for nature and helped him combine it with his love of science.

He spent half his junior year of college in Madrid, Spain, working with the avian research and conservation organization SEO/BirdLife—which demanded he learn fluent Spanish. He researched his senior thesis on spotted knapweed, a fast-growing and poisonous European plant with pink flowers that has invaded Minnesota's prairies, dunes, and pine barrens, investigating its effect on local bee species. (Turns out it didn't hurt the bees at all—though it harms plenty of other species, especially native plants the fast-growing weed crowds out.)

"I knew I belonged outside," Jared realized.

But until he arrived at Fisi Camp in Masai Mara last June 22, he'd never before had to deal with the ever-changing demands of remote fieldwork: fixing flashlights. Hauling drinking water. Rushing an injured Masai herdsman to a clinic. He learned to change a tire for the first time. "Every day brings surprises," he says. "No two days are the same—ever!"

And one more thing he's learned: "To most people, a muddy hyena might be ugly. But really look at her. Look at her ears. Look at her eyes. Each is truly individual, the behavior of each is very distinctive. Some are great mothers. Some are terrible. Some are always found together, like best friends.

"Even if the common knowledge says an animal is boring, or greedy, or ugly," he says, "if you love it, that's all the more reason you should study it!"

Once he leaves Kenya, he's headed to graduate school, where he'll study the social behavior of dolphins in Shark Bay, Australia.

Jared stores biological samples in liquid nitrogen.

Otis surveys the rain-swept plains of Masai Mara.

CHAPTER FIVE

Kinda See 'Em

The ground is too soft from rain to drive off-track, so it's a couple of days before we can go out for more obs. Finally, at three thirty on a Friday afternoon, Kay decides that she, Dee, Amy, Nic, Lawi, and I can finally venture out, "just to see what we might find."

What we find, by 4:04, are three female and two male lions, lying in the shade of an acacia. One lioness licks her paw, while another rolls onto her back languidly in the heat, legs in the air, as if asking for a belly rub. Better not!

A lion catnaps in the grass.

But while all the tourists want to see the "big, dumb blondes," as Dee calls the lions, we want hyenas. "There's twenty hyenas lying out there in the grass," promises Kay. "We just can't see them yet."

Half-past four: Big chestnut and charcoal-colored antelopes called topi, delicate little gold, black, and white Thompson's gazelles, and powerful, spiral-horned impalas graze beneath sun-streaked clouds. Two male ostrich stroll by on pinkish legs, lifting their

Topi.

Thompson's gazelles are alert and fast, but hyenas often hunt them.

two-toed feet as delicately as ballerinas. A single male wildebeest, his black mane and light beard hanging like fringe from his neck and chin, calls *gnnnnnnnnnnu!*

"Between the topi and the impala," Lawi asks, "is that a hyena?"

Kay peers through her binoculars. Nope. Warthog. "We've been fooled many a time by warthogs." Finding hyenas isn't as easy as it might seem.

We drive on, heading along the track to a pond called Magi Fisi—Hyena Water in Swahili. "They often lounge in the shallows," explains Kay. But all we find are two jackals.

We scan the horizon with binoculars for three minutes. Cape buffalo, topi, elephants, and a glowering sky. Thunder rumbles. We see it's raining on Kay's more remote Serena Fisi Camp. But on the opposite side of the reserve our camp still looks dry.

5:01 p.m.: "Is that a hyena?" asks Nic.

"It sure is!" Kay answers.

"It's two!" cries Amy. "One is collared!" And this adult has a distinctive notch on the right ear. It's a female, born in late July 2008, named Tilt—and the other hyena, now grooming the first hyena's right rear leg, is probably her son, Otis, born in January 2015. Kay hasn't seen them for a while. She wonders what they've been up to.

A puddle bath is one way to keep cool.

Tilt walks twenty yards and lies down in the heat, while the young male scratches his neck with his left rear foot. But now, at 5:08, another car has appeared. Because our car has stopped, the tourists and their guide assume we are looking at something interesting, and they want to see, too.

"They think we've found a lion," Dee says.

Tilt and her youngster stand up at the car's approach. Seeing the animals are "only" hyenas, the tourist car moves on. But for us, things are just starting to get interesting.

Another hyena approaches from the northeast. It comes within thirty yards of one of the grazing impalas—good hyena food. But the antelope doesn't even lift his head to look at the predator. "Sometimes they really tense up when a hyena approaches, and sometimes they're really blasé," says Kay. "We don't know what signals they're reading."

"Another hyena at ten o'clock," Dee calls from the back seat. She's referring to the position on the face of a clock—near the front left side of our car.

"How far away?" asks Kay.

"Way far," answers Dee. But it's clear that hyenas are starting to converge here. They may be approaching a den.

This is especially interesting for Kay. We are now near the most distant denning area, to the north and west of camp, in the territory of a mysterious group of the Talek West Clan, "the group we know least about," because they hang out in dense thickets of croton bushes. They're called the "KCM" group—which stands for "kinda see 'em." Anything we can learn today will be valuable.

"We don't know what's going on with their dens," says Kay. The researchers think there are dens somewhere in the dense bushes ahead of us. But those bushes encompass dozens of acres. Kay would love to know where the KCM den is. If one of the hyenas we see is a mom—and we can tell if her teats are swollen with milk for nursing her babies—"we'd do well to follow her," says Kay. She could lead us, at last, to the Mystery Den.

We follow the hyena Dee has spotted with her binoculars. The animal crosses the road, now about three hundred yards ahead of us. "Yep," Kay pronounces at five thirty p.m., "she's a female. I saw nipples." We turn the car around and slowly creep after her.

"I think it's Harpy," Kay says, noting a distinctive scar on her neck—a healed area over what looks like a lump on her throat. Harpy was born October 29, 2009, and her family is ranked fifth out of the fourteen maternal lineages in Talek West. Her last known cub, Unagi, was born in March 2014. "She could easily have new cubs," Kay says. "Lawi, do you think you can keep her in sight?"

We turn. It's 5:36—soon to be dark—and the area is marshy. We can't follow her directly or we risk getting stuck again—this time, in the dark, surrounded by lions and hyenas. "If we turn down this road, maybe she'll cross in front of us," Kay suggests.

But we lose her. She vanishes into the tall grass.

At 5:39, Kay suggests "Let's stop and scan." Kay stands, poking her head through the pop-top roof of the Land Cruiser, and slowly sweeps the green landscape with her magnified gaze, looking for a bump, a dark spot, the rounded shape of an ear. We all do the same. "Anybody see her?"

No. So we cruise.

5:41: A hyena in the grass! Lawi backs up the car while the animal stares at us with clear, shimmering eyes. Is it Harpy?

No. It's a different animal. But three minutes later, Lawi spots another hyena. And the next second, "There's two!" says Amy. "Three!" calls Kay. But they're just snoozing, not heading to the den. We drive slowly forward, listening to the bubbling sound of frogs and the swirl of the wind. Lawi spots yet another hyena by the road, hunched to take a poop. "It could be her," says Kay. "Let's take a look."

Alas, it's not Harpy. The hyena finishes pooping and now proceeds toward a new

Kay watches Harpy as she disappears into the grass.

hyena, who approaches from the west. The pooper greets the newcomer with an open mouth, ears back, acknowledging the new hyena's higher rank. In response, the newcomer lies down and raises a leg to expose her belly, revealing the prominent nipples of a nursing mother. In a dog, lying down and rolling over is a sign of submission. But in hyenas, explains Kay, the one who lies down is dominant, "as if she can't even be bothered to stand up." The pooper sniffs the mother's undercarriage and licks her nipples. The dominant animal then opens her mouth wide, as if in a yawn, and shakes her head. "There's signal value in that," says Kay, "but we don't know what it is."

More mysteries. But the most pressing question is: are the hyenas we are watching just resting, or are they getting ready to go hunting—or to visit the Mystery Den?

Kay notes that the rain over Serena has started to move near our camp. We might have to leave before the rain makes the tracks too muddy to return. Too bad; this time of evening, on the cusp of dark, "is the time hyenas typically get together before they *do* something," says Kay.

"I'm sorry we didn't find Harpy," says Kay. "She should have new babies by now. If she were beelining that way, the den might be in those miserable bushes . . ."

Before she can finish her sentence, another hyena approaches us from the opposite side of the road. And it's Harpy!

Now hyenas seem to be coming in from everywhere. Another approaches from the east. Yet a different one walks in from the northeast. If these are new mothers, they are likely all headed to the same place: the Mystery Den.

At 6:10 Harpy heads into the bushes. She weaves right, then left—"just to psych us out!" jokes Amy. She may be hunting for baby gazelles, which their mothers leave hiding, motionless, in the grass. Harpy zigzags this way and that, weaving in and out of our view in the tall grass. And then up pop the heads of two subadult hyenas, their rounded ears barely visible above the tall grass. The Mystery Den is almost certainly very near.

When they meet, the lower-ranked hyena opens her mouth in appeasement. Then the dominant hyena lies down to expose her belly.

But so is the rain. The skies are heavy and thunder is brewing in the fading light. "Oh, that looks like a lot of water going to fall tonight," says Dee.

Harpy disappears into the bushes, reappears behind a patch of grass—and then is gone. "I can find that place where she vanished," says Kay. "We'll come back when it's drier."

We're disappointed to leave Harpy and her undiscovered cubs. But it's been a surprisingly successful outing nonetheless: "Now," Dee rejoices with Kay, "we'll finally be able to find that den!"

AMY'S STORY

The newest member of camp, quiet, slender Amy, arrived in Masai Mara in April. With her blue eyes framed in big red glasses (her favorite color), she looks like she could be a writer—and she is one, with a fantasy novel just accepted for publication. But animals have been her love since childhood.

She grew up on a cul-de-sac in Victorville, California, a tomboy digging in the dirt looking for bugs. She cared for a succession of pet snails, as well as a cat, several dogs, mice, fish, and a hamster. She found animals easy to understand, even though they don't speak. Her sister, Kristy, has autism, and she doesn't speak much, either, "but she is very expressive," Amy explains. "I wouldn't be who I am without my sister."

As a kid, Amy read books to expand her world, and her favorites were about animals: Jean Craighead George's *My Side of the Mountain*, Gary Paulsen's *Winterdance*, Jack London's *The Call of the Wild*. Summers, she enjoyed attending weeklong camps with wildlife themes. At one, she was kissed by a beluga whale. At another, the best part was getting a starfish caught in her hair. It seemed natural to go on to college and major in wildlife biology. At Humboldt State University in California, she learned to gently capture birds in nets, conducted research on the raccoons on campus, and ventured out in an inflatable Zodiac boat following sea lions and gray whales.

Because she'd always wanted to go to Africa, she was intrigued at the end of her freshman year to learn about an eight-week opportunity to study African carnivores in Kenya—with Kay Holekamp! But she was too young to apply—the job was for juniors and seniors. Instead, she studied fishers—large, handsome members of the weasel family—in the Northern Sierras that summer. After her sophomore year, she landed an internship at Michigan State University, where Kay was one of the professors. Amy was entranced with hyenas and hoped she'd work with Kay. But Amy was paired instead with a researcher studying honeybees—animals she knew little about, but soon grew to admire: they communicate chemically and with a "waggle dance" that shows others the way to nectar sources. At the end of that summer, Amy finally met Kay, and soon tried again. She applied for an eight-week program the following summer with Kay's Michigan lab. But she didn't get accepted.

Instead, Amy spent that summer working at Wolf Education and Research Center in Idaho. She reapplied for Kay's hyena program after her senior year—by then it was a yearlong position. She was a finalist for the job—but didn't get it. She had hedged her bets and was accepted for three other positions elsewhere for which she'd also applied. Among those options, she chose a three-month position at the Wild Spirit Wolf Sanctuary in New Mexico. But Kay urged her to keep in touch.

Just a week later, Kay emailed her with a question: "Would you be interested in coming in March 2016?"

You bet she would! She arrived in Kenya that March and got to Masai Mara in April.

At times, it seemed like everything was conspiring to prevent Amy from going to Africa to study hyenas with Kay. But now, Amy sees the situation was exactly the opposite: "If I'd been accepted the first time I applied to work for Kay, I'd not have had these other opportunities." She'd have missed out on learning about animal communication in bees; she'd never have worked with the wolves in New Mexico. And while waiting to join Kay in Africa, Amy took a temporary position as a field crew leader though Montana State University, leading undergraduates collecting coyote and wolf vocalizations at Yellowstone.

The way she sees it, all these other opportunities helped prepare her for this assignment, here with the wild hyenas of Masai Mara. "Everything," Amy now understands, "has led me to here."

Amy spins blood samples in the centrifuge.

CHAPTER SIX

Clan War

It's too marshy to return to the Mystery Den, so today we have another objective in mind: darting, examining, and possibly radio-collaring one of the young male hyenas who's just on the verge of leaving his family.

Females inherit their mother's territories and social position, but young males' fates are less certain. Until they leave home, they enjoy the privileges of their mothers' rank. Along with their sisters, the sons of high-ranking moms get quick access to the best food. Others in their clan defer to them. Cubs "graduate" from the den at around nine months old and begin to hunt with the family; after age two, most young males set out to find a new clan to join. And in any new clan, these young males are the lowest-ranking members of all—even the sons of queens like BUAR. That seems like a raw deal. "Why," Kay asks, "would the male son of an alpha female give up his fantastic position and such good access to food, only to be discriminated against in a new clan?"

One reason is surely that sons who stay with their mothers, sisters, and aunts would have nobody to mate with other than family—and inbreeding creates genetic disasters. (Human royalty who unwisely failed to avoid this problem produced offspring like Mad King Ludwig II of Bavaria, Juana the Mad of Castile, Charles the Mad of France . . . you get the idea.) But spotted hyena sons may still enjoy certain benefits of their high-ranking mothers even after leaving home. So far, Kay and her students have radio-collared eleven high-ranking and nine low-ranking dispersing males. Preliminary evidence suggests that even though the young males rank low on the social ladder of their new clans, those whose mothers were high ranking are more confident. "They don't grovel hysterically," says

Kay. And a German team studying hyenas in nearby Tanzania's Serengeti found that sons of high-ranking females sire more young, and their offspring are more likely to survive. As for the sons of low-ranking mothers? In Kay's study, not one of the nine low-ranking males her team radio-collared is still alive.

In search of young males, we head out at five thirty a.m. in two cars—Kay, Benson, Nic, and me in one, and Amy, Dee, and Ciara in the other. (Jared has gone to Nairobi.) Whoever sees a good darting candidate will radio or text the other.

"I feel the best darting opportunity is going to be between Maji Fisi and the KCM area and the den," says Kay. Location is crucial for darting, and not only because we don't want to get stuck in the mud. We need to stay clear of lions, for they will attack a compromised hyena. We must avoid water, or the darted hyena might stagger into it before the drug takes full effect and drown. And we can't dart where another hyena might see us. They'd remember the event and avoid the researchers for years.

So Kay chooses an area where she's often seen hyenas lying singly near or in the road.

"I don't want to get my hopes up," says Kay, who's driving today. But clearly, we all want to dart a hyena very much—especially

Benson records the coordinates of a telemetry reading.

Benson, who is Kay's best shot with the tranquilizer gun. Each chance to get this close to a live hyena offers a terrific opportunity: even without radio-collaring it, the chance to weigh, measure, and sample blood, feces, and glandular secretions yields crucial new information on hyena growth, health, hormones, and the effect of rank.

As dawn approaches, the songs of bats and frogs start to mix with the pulsing coo of doves. In the dim light, we're greeted with the sight of three lions. "Well, we're not darting anywhere near here today," says Kay. We move on.

Five giraffes stand silhouetted against the morning. A topi lies propped up on his chest, chewing the cud from his rumen, one of his four stomachs. A safari balloon has launched, hissing loudly overhead. We hope it won't scare away the hyenas.

"See anyone, Benson?" asks Kay.

"No, no one."

"Rats."

But Benson can scan with telemetry to see if any radio-collared hyenas are in the area, even if they aren't candidates for darting. It's always important to see which hyenas are where, and when. Benson dons the earphones and readies the recording equipment for his observations. "Helios and BUAR are coming in," he says. They're around, but obscured from sight by bushes.

At 6:56, Benson spots what might be the perfect quarry: a young hyena lying quietly by the road. He's so calm he doesn't even rise as we drive over for a better look; he only lifts his head and sniffs.

"This is one mellow animal!" remarks Kay. But who is it? I pass her the ID book. The V on his neck identifies him as BOU—a young male, soon to leave his home den for a new clan. BOU had been darted once before,

when he was younger, for a hormone assay. But since this hyena is a dispersing male, he'd be ideal for radio telemetry.

There's one issue: only cubs two and a half years or older can wear the collars. Because they're still growing, a snug collar could choke them if applied too young. Checking the ID book, Kay is disappointed. BOU was born March 2014—at two years, two months, "He's still too young."

We reunite with some of Kay's old favorites on this day. In the morning, we catch up with Helios again. We encounter Parcheesi—Twister's sister (both named after board games). But why aren't they together as usual? We spot Nassau, a male, his face bloody from a recent meal. We visit Baez as she nurses her two cubs in the cool of the morning at the den. A lovely, peaceful scene—but not the one we're looking for.

"Doesn't anyone see a hyena we can dart today?" asks Kay in exasperation. But Ciara and Amy haven't either, or they'd have alerted us. And now our time has run out. The blood study requires that samples be collected in the morning, because hormone values change throughout the day; to get consistent comparisons, any blood collected must be processed before ten a.m.

Lions attack hyenas, given the chance. The two are competitors for prey.

Amazon nurses her cubs.

We head back disappointed. But as we turn toward camp, Masai Mara gives us a consolation prize for our frustrating morning: a party of three bushy-maned, adult male lions, three lionesses, and a cub. Two of the males rub heads in greeting. They are probably brothers. The other male looks at us with golden eyes, his mane swept by the wind and backlit by the sun. It seems that, here in the Mara, there's always a surprise just around the corner.

We leave at five for afternoon obs. Kay, Ciara, Nic, and I take one vehicle. Benson, Amy, and Dee take the other. They'll conduct a survey of the illegal livestock they can spot while driving along a standard route in the park, a routine chore performed twice monthly. (The highest tally: 28,000 illegal animals counted in one night.) We'll head out to a place between Maji Fisi and a swampy area called Horseshoe Lugga, hoping for some action.

As usual, Ciara notes all the carnivores along our route, from the eleven banded mongooses we spot just as we leave camp to the adult male lion we spot half an hour later. Ciara tunes in to "Radio Fisi": Helios is coming in on channel 1171. But soon we spot a

hyena sacked out behind a croton bush. It's Amazon, nursing cubs POW and Urc. We move the car for a better view, but the cubs skitter down into the den, frightened. For a hyena cub, the den is even more comforting than Mom. The den is the safest place on earth, where in the narrow tunnels, only a python—or another cub—can reach them. Once Kay saw a lion sit on top of a den for an

hour and stick a front leg down into the den, trying to reach a cub. But the babies stayed safe.

We watch the cubs and their mom in delight as the sun begins its drop from the sky. And then, at 6:23, the excitement begins.

Two hyenas greet in the middle of the road, saluting with a rear leg held high, each sniffing the other. Then out of the grass pop four more. It's a group of six—no, seven. "Wait! There's more!" cries Ciara. We can't keep up with the action, it's happening so fast!

Six more hyenas lope in from the north. Four wear radio collars. Everyone is excited. Tails bristle. Hyenas giggle with tension. They zigzag. They chase. A wave of hyenas rushes one way, then turns and rushes the opposite direction.

This can only mean one thing: it's a clan war!

Everyone scrambles to identify who's who, to make sense of what's happening. In a clan war, a group of hyenas band together to defend their hunting territory from another group by chasing the others away. That's exactly what we see unfolding before us. Hair raised, amid excited whoops and stressed-out giggles, two groups of hyenas are racing, en masse, toward and then away from one another.

But here we see no foreign invaders. They are all members of the same Talek West Clan!

Soon it's clear that members of the group that dens at Dave's Den, including BUAR, Helios, Decimeter, and Twister, are chasing and attacking the group that hangs out at Lucky Leopard Den. The Lucky Leopard crew lopes west in retreat; the Dave's Den group wanders, sniffs the ground, and carefully marks their territory with a pasty secretion from a gland beneath the tail. We turn to try to find and identify all the members of the retreating party.

Then we hear whooping to the north! Eight more hyenas are arriving. No—nine. Wait—ten! We abandon the search for the Lucky Leopard Den members to investigate the new group. Who are they? There are thirteen hyenas in all—and everyone is from the Kinda See 'Em group, whose Mystery Den we had nearly located the evening before.

It's over in a flash. "Oh my gosh, I can't believe what just happened!" says Ciara. She's only seen one event remotely like this in a year of almost daily observations. Kay has seen more, but is still thrilled—and still trying to make sense of the implications.

The hyenas chase each other back and forth until one clan retreats.

A lone hyena heads home after the excitement.

The whole clan war took place in just four minutes. Luckily, Benson, Amy, and Dee, in the other car, saw it too. Back at camp, we'll compare notes. Who was seen, and with which group? Where will the new boundaries be drawn? Which group or groups will end up with the best territories? What will that mean for the survival of the family members in the different groups?

"A spur-of-the-moment thing like this shows you something that's been brewing for a long time," Kay explains. The clan is splitting into rival factions. "It's a very dynamic situation right now," she explains. "At Dave's Den, it's been standing room only for a long time. Sometimes there's no space to lie down with your cub! So the group will need to split." And throughout the year, her researchers have seen KCMers and the group from Lucky Leopard Den switch back and forth— one group in one area, and then another day, in the other. But the splitting groups had not been seen engaged in all-out war—until tonight.

To think that until dusk, we had thought this was a disappointing day! "After years of waiting for the gigantic Talek West Clan to divide, it takes something like this to confirm it," Kay says. "These clan fission events are incredibly rare to see. For us, tonight was tremendously important."

BENSON'S STORY

"Hyenas," Benson says, "changed my life." This is true of Kay and Dee and the other research assistants as well. But for Benson, the change has been the most profound of all.

When Benson was three years old, his dad—a herder—died of malaria, a fever transmitted by mosquitoes. An uncle and his wives took him in, along with his dad's two wives (like many of the characters in the Bible, Masai men often marry several women) and Benson's two younger brothers and two older sisters. As a boy, Benson attended elementary school on weekdays, and then came home to care for the family's goats, sheep, and cows. As a young herder, Benson learned a lot about wild animals, because he saw them every day. He learned to climb trees when a Cape buffalo would chase him. He learned which snakes were dangerous. He learned about the weather: the shapes of the clouds and what they meant, the smell of the soil when rain is coming.

Benson wanted to go to high school, but high school isn't free in Kenya, and his uncle's family had no money. So he went to work. He welcomed tourists to a Masai-themed tourist camp in Talek, where visitors would learn about Masai culture. But he remained interested in animals and the natural world. Whenever he saw a new bird, plant, or bug, he'd look it up, learn its name. He enjoyed speaking with tourists, and the English he'd started learning in elementary school improved. He learned to

drive a car. He dreamed of finding a job involving wildlife—perhaps as a tourist guide.

In 2010, Benson came to work at Fisi Camp, assisting the cook, Joseph. Kay was then in Michigan. He made friends with research assistants and graduate students, and often asked them about their work. He became fascinated with hyenas. Most Masai don't like them, he admits: "People in my village, they aren't liking hyenas, because they steal things at night. When they come to the *boma* at night, you have to come quickly with your spear." But the more he learned about hyenas, the more he liked them. "I like how they socialize, how they share dens, eat together, maintain rank. I like identifying them. I like the clan membership. I like knowing all the mother hyena's kids, and who is related to who."

Soon the other researchers in camp were taking the curious Benson along with them on obs. One day they came upon a hyena who had been killed by a lion. Benson assisted them with the necropsy (as an animal autopsy is called). Everyone was impressed with his care, skill, and knowledge. When Kay arrived in camp that May, she urged him to apply as a research assistant. He started working in the position two months later.

Benson is a great shot with the dart gun.

Now even bigger changes are afoot for Benson. In the next few months, though he's never been to high school, he is taking the high school equivalency exam in order to apply for college in the United States. He will take his wife and his two young sons, ages four and eight months, with him.

"If I wasn't here, I wouldn't think of getting more education," Benson says. "The hyenas are attracting me to a lot of changes. A lot of students are coming. They are much educated—and I am thinking, maybe me, too! I am looking forward to going to school—and my boys going to school. Education is the backbone of everything—and I want my children and grandchildren to succeed."

The team prepares to measure and sample McDonald's.

CHAPTER SEVEN

The Capture of McDonald's

Five thirty a.m. comes fast on the heels of last night's excitement. But we're still hoping to dart a young male. Maybe it will happen this morning. "I think our better targets will be to the north and west," Kay says as we pack up the gear.

When we leave, the moon is still veiled in clouds. But Benson manages to spot two jackals in the dark. He and Kay scan with binoculars, looking for the lions we saw yesterday. They've moved on.

By six thirty we arrive at Dave's Den. Not much action. "They're so exhausted from all the excitement last night, the hyenas must be sleeping," says Kay.

We drive on. Nine ostrich stroll by, the male's fluffy black and white wing feathers bouncing and jostling like the bustle on a lady's dress.

At 7:01, Benson spots a young hyena walking slowly in the tall grass. It's McDonald's, says Benson—a son of Burger (which is why the grad students named the babies after fast food joints). A high-ranking female, Burger

hangs out with the KCM group, and was one of the hyenas involved in the clan war the night before.

"Is this one who needs to be darted?" asks Kay. We consult the hyena yearbook. McDonald's was born in the first week of December 2014—so he's too small to be radio-collared. But his blood should be assayed and his body measured and weighed. This is the perfect opportunity.

"Let's see if we can lure him out of the tall grass," suggests Kay—to afford Benson a better shot. To do so, Kay has packed two of the hyenas' favorite treats: powdered milk and popcorn.

McDonald's has never seen popcorn before, and he ignores the white kernels Benson scatters out the window. But powdered

Sticky-whiskered cubs like milk powder.

milk is another story. Kay discovered that hyenas love this calorie-rich, healthy food, so she uses it to teach the cubs to approach her research vehicles (which they can tell from other cars) to lick it off the ground. It comes in handy when you need a hyena to stand up so you can check its spot pattern, or to move someone to a better area for darting. Benson sprinkles some powder on the shorter grass in front of us, and Kay backs the car off. McDonald's comes to sniff the treat and begins to eat it eagerly. Benson now has a clear view of the hyena out the car's passenger window. He is only ten yards away. "So what do you think,

Benson? Want to make up a dart?" Kay suggests quietly.

Nic and I pass Benson the Tupperware container with the supplies: syringe, sleeve, needle, dart, fletch, and the vial of tranquilizer, Telazol. As the needle pierces the animal's skin, the sleeve gets pushed back off the holes in the needle, which then delivers the drug. Benson measures 2.2 cubic centimeters from the vial of Telazol into the syringe, and loads it into the dart. Nic and I slowly, quietly open the gun case and pass forward the barrel, then the stock. Benson loads the dart into the barrel and attaches the stock while Kay texts Amy, Ciara, and Dee in the other vehicle. "If he goes down, we'll need help," she says. She hopes they'll be in cell phone range.

Benson prepares a dart.

We're tense while McDonald's finishes eating the powdered milk. Another hyena could come by and ruin our darting opportunity. A lion could show up. A tour vehicle could come. Or a loud, hissing safari balloon . . .

Benson rolls down the window, takes aim, and fires. Unlike the loud blasts from guns Laurence Frank used in his earlier hyena study, this one makes only a soft popping sound. It's a perfect shot. Kay sets the timer to see when the drug kicks in. It's 7:41 a.m.

The sharp, slender needle probably stings like a tsetse fly bite. McDonald's sits down, glances at his flank. He spots the dart's red fluffy fletch and yanks it out with his teeth—but the needle has already delivered the drug. Then McDonald's walks toward the car, looking for more milk. Soon his hind legs wobble. His front legs buckle. By seven forty-five, McDonald's is propped up on his forefeet, his head weaving drunkenly. He licks his lips.

"Go to sleep, little guy," Kay says softly.

We wait in silence. Who knows what McDonald's is experiencing? He won't remember. Telazol has an amnesia-producing component, like many anesthetics used in human medicine. But still, Kay wants to keep the moment as calm as possible. The only sounds are the songs of the sparrows and the sigh of the wind.

Benson takes careful aim with the dart gun.

Six minutes and thirteen seconds after darting, McDonald's is asleep. Kay pulls the car up beside him. With perfect timing, Amy, Ciara, and Dee arrive in the other vehicle.

Kay gently rolls McDonald's onto his right side, protects his open eyes with a moist and soothing gel, and covers them with a purple flowered pillowcase. Eight minutes after the darting, she is already drawing vials of blood from his neck for hormone and DNA studies. Meanwhile, Amy and Ciara begin measurements of his body. They softly announce each measurement, while Dee, repeating each number carefully, logs the information on the data sheet. They start with the skull:

Zygomatic arch (the cheekbone, under the eye) to top of crest (the ridge to which chewing muscles attach), 12 cm.

Back of eye to base of ear, 7.6 cm.

Ear length, 9.2 cm.

Skull length, from top of nose to under notch (at back of skull), 24 cm.

Head circumference, 46.3 cm. . . .

In six minutes, Kay finishes drawing eight vials of blood. "I'm going to get swabs ready," she announces. While the others continue taking measurements, Kay withdraws a surgical spatula—a tiny, sterile spoon—from its packaging in medical kit to take a sample of what she calls "hyena butter"—the pasty

secretion from special glands under the tail with which hyenas mark their territories. She lets me take a whiff. It smells strongly of musk, but not unpleasantly, like a stable with thousands of flowers thrown in. Each clan's secretions are chemically different. It's full of information for other hyenas: who left it, to which family he or she belonged, and likely the age, sex, and reproductive condition of the animal who marked his or her territory with the secretion. Now scientists can begin to learn this information, too.

The measurements continue:

Right front foot length, 20 cm.

Upper leg length, 25.7 cm.

Dee checks McDonald's body for ticks and scars. She finds a few ticks, but no healed injuries. Because he's the son of a high-ranking mom, nobody dares mess with him.

Benson uses calipers to measure McDonald's impressive teeth, tooth by tooth. "Lower canine?" Kay asks. "25.7 millimeters," Benson replies, and continues.

While Benson works with McDonald's head, Kay works on his other end. She swabs his anus and penis, and stores the swabs in sterile vials. Hyenas' every secretion is grounds for study. She moves forward and takes a swab from his nostrils. Everyone works gently, quietly, quickly. Nobody wants to have to give the hyena another dose of Telazol, because that would mean he'd recover more slowly—with more danger that a lion or rival hyena might find him.

The crew rolls McDonald's to his other side to complete the measurements. Ciara removes the darting needle and swabs the small puncture with Betadine to prevent infection. At 8:20, only one measurement remains. The crew rolls McDonald's onto a stretcher and weighs him on the portable scale: subtracting the weight of the stretcher, he's 32.9 kilos, or 72.5 pounds. He's fat and healthy!

Benson and Ciara lift the hyena on the stretcher and load him into the back of the Land Cruiser like a patient in an ambulance. I'll ride in back with him to make sure his head doesn't bang against the hard floor on the bumpy ride to his release site, and to keep his eyes covered. I can't help but gently stroke the unconscious hyena's fur. It's softest in back of the ears. Though McDonald's is just a youngster, I'm in awe of his huge feet, his massive jaws.

Kay has chosen a release site carefully. We can see it, just across a creek, in a thicket of croton bushes. It's a no man's land, belonging to none of the fissioning families, well shaded and well hidden from anyone who might bother a recovering animal. But because it's across the creek, it'll take fifteen to twenty minutes to drive there—on corrugated roads. During which, I realize, I'll be confined in the back of a cramped space with a live hyena.

We start moving. I do my best to keep McDonald's head from banging. But the track is so bumpy that his head bounces off the stretcher. I cradle his head in one hand while sliding Kay's dark blue polar fleece beneath it as a pillow. But still, with each jolt, his heavy head bounces, and it's all I can do to keep it from sliding off the pillow with one hand while using the other to hold the bandanna over his eyes.

Then McDonald's begins to move his head on his own. I realize with alarm that a hyena is waking up in my lap.

"I'm afraid of his head bouncing too much," I say to Kay. We stop the car and she takes a look. "He's doing fine. It's okay," she says. We resume the journey.

I'm stroking McDonald's and trying to cradle his head. I'm worried about him, and I'm worried about me. I trust Kay's advice completely, but can't help remembering a story she told me the night before at dinner: one of the female hyenas at the California research facility was giving birth. She had been hand-raised as a cub, and as she gave birth, her human caretaker was there, stroking her gently from outside the bars of the animal's enclosure. Suddenly, the hyena, surely in terrible pain, turned her head, snapped through the bars, and chomped her caretaker's hand in half. Doctors had to remove one of the woman's big toes to fashion a digit to replace her missing thumb.

We hit another big bump. "Hold on!" says Kay—and we hit another. McDonald's lifts his huge head off the makeshift pillow, twists his neck, opens his jaws.

Poor McDonald's! Coming out of anesthetic can be disorienting for a human in a hospital. Imagine a hyena who comes to inside a *car*!

With bump after bump, the hyena in my lap seems to be jolted increasingly awake. Now a front paw twitches. A rear leg kicks out. "I'm not liking this!" I call to Kay in the front. We stop the car and Benson replaces my position, while I lean over from a back seat. It takes the two of us to keep McDonald's big head still, and his eyes covered, for the final, bone-rattling minutes of the ride.

At last, we arrive at the croton thicket. Nic and Benson carry McDonald's stretcher to an area of deep shade. We roll him off the stretcher onto soft leaf litter beneath a large, shady bush, out of sight from prying eyes, where he'll be cool and comfortable. Quickly we gather fallen branches to surround him with a low pen, just big enough to restrain him from wandering drunkenly about as he gets up—which would attract dangerous attention from lions and rival hyenas. As we work, McDonald's tries spasmodically to rise.

McDonald's is left in a sheltered spot to recover.

"Everybody, get away," says Kay. He's no danger to us, she promises. He won't actually be able to stand for another thirty minutes. But she doesn't want him to associate us with anything scary or unpleasant, so we won't stick around to watch his recovery. We're confident he's safe. He's a strong, healthy, young male hyena on the cusp of adulthood, blessed with the great good luck of being born to a high-ranking mother. "He should be just fine," says Kay. "That couldn't have gone better!"

Sy looks after McDonald's in the vehicle.

A SKULL LIKE A SWISS ARMY KNIFE

Sitting at a desk in front of her tent, Kay cradles the sun-bleached skull of an adult male hyena. She describes it as "a powerful tool for breaking open bones and eating really fast." Everything about the skull tells that story: Massive muscles to power the jaws' tremendous force cause a bulge in the top back of the head. "You can see where they attach here," says Kay. And look at the "roof" of the skull: like a cathedral, it's vaulted, to dissipate the force of bone-cracking. Otherwise the tremendous force of opening the skeleton of its prey might crack the hyena's own skull! With its thick bones, massive muscles, and huge teeth, an adult hyena's head can weigh fifteen to eighteen pounds. (The head of a grown human, whose body weighs about as much as a hyena's, might weigh ten.)

The hyena's large teeth are specialized for different jobs, like the different blades of a Swiss Army knife. Incisors rip. Canines pierce. Another set is particularly designed for cracking bones (and from wear on one of these teeth—known as P-3—you can tell not only a hyena's age, but what side he or she liked best to chew on). The back of the mouth is full of shearing teeth like sewing shears. Compare this, suggests Kay, with the teeth of a lion: though the long, pointy canines are impressive, most of a lion's teeth are pretty similar to one another: "Which is why a lion licks his food all day!" notes Kay.

A hyena doesn't have that luxury. A lion might steal a hyena's rightful kill. That's why these hunters need a skull like this: to be able to bring down, kill, and eat an animal as big as a wildebeest in under thirty minutes. Kay is still in awe of it: "That is one heck of a skull, man!"

CHAPTER EIGHT

Glimpses and Revelations

While we're releasing McDonald's, Ciara, Dee, and Amy rush back to camp with the precious samples, eager to prepare the blood so it can be safely stored without its components degrading. By the time we return, our dining table has been transformed into a lab bench. Covered with newspaper, the table is set now not with plates and condiments, but with data sheets, labels, glass pipettes, and test tubes of blood standing tall like giraffes in their Styrofoam racks. Small cryovials, special test tubes for storing biological material at low temperatures, stand ready to receive prepared samples for storage in liquid nitrogen, until they can be shipped back to the lab in Michigan.

A centrifuge hums like a blender while everyone helps prepare and label samples. Some of the blood is spun immediately to separate its components—plasma, serum, and white blood cells—and each component is then stored in a separate tube. Other samples sit for two hours to separate the components a different way. It all depends on what kind of test will be conducted with the samples when they get back to Michigan: some tests will look at hormones, chemical messengers that help cells communicate with one another in the body;

others will look at antibodies, blood proteins that fight infection; yet others sequence genes, segments of DNA, the blueprints for life. One study will look at genes to reveal who McDonald's father is, which would otherwise be a mystery. Everyone is busy preparing tubes and recording data.

Samples like these have already yielded intriguing new information. For instance: Members of the Talek West Clan show higher levels of stress hormones, like cortisol, than those of the Serena Clan. Why? Possibly because of Talek West's closer proximity to

Masai herders. Immigrant males show high levels of the male sex hormone testosterone. But when males stay home with the family, even if they're the same age as the immigrants, their testosterone levels are much lower. Does this lessen the danger of inbreeding by reducing their interest in mating or by making them less attractive to females—or both?

Even the samples of "hyena butter" hold surprising secrets. The composition of this important scent gland secretion in the Talek West Clan is markedly different from Talek East's—even though the two clans are descended from the same ancestors. Like the human gut, the hyena's scent gland is full of harmless (and often helpful) tiny organisms. (Our gut, like the hyena's scent gland, is a habitat for these creatures; that's why scientists call them both "microbiomes.") At only two or three weeks of age, baby hyenas start "pasting" plant stalks, even though their scent glands don't have any paste yet. How and when do they acquire their clan's unique microorganisms? How do these microbial organisms influence the chemical messages hyenas leave on grass stalks? One of Kay's grad students is trying to find out.

Other students are investigating patterns of gene expression from DNA collected from blood samples. Kay explains, "genes get turned on and off, with profound effects on how you look and how you act." How do genes the hyenas are born with interact with their upbringing—the quality of their food, their mother's rank? How does this affect a baby hyena's personality development?

The samples McDonald's provided the group today are treasures. "Did you notice that the very first thing that went into the car the night of the flood was the liquid nitrogen with its samples," says Kay, "and the data? Those are the most precious things here—besides people's lives."

Everyone is eager to check on McDonald's to make sure he recovered in peace. That eve-

Everything is cataloged and stored.

ning, we find the little corral we built in the shade has been opened from the inside, suggesting he woke up and is back to his hyena business as usual.

We'd love to find him to see for ourselves that he's fine. (And in fact, days later, after Nic and I leave, the group sees him, healthy and unafraid of the research vehicles, as if nothing had happened.) But it's extremely difficult to find an individual hyena if the animal isn't radio-collared. In fact, in field studies, much of the time, it's difficult to accomplish any specific goal, like finding a certain animal, on a particular day. "That's one thing being here in Africa teaches you," notes Dee. "You can't control what happens. You can only control how you behave, how you react."

The one thing a researcher can control: you can show up. Comedian and director Woody Allen once said that 80 percent of success springs from "just showing up." That's true of fieldwork: success comes with day after patient day of simply being there and observing, waiting for a moment of revelation.

At 7:52 a.m. while we're on morning obs at Dave's Den, Ciara gets a cell phone call from a grad student based at Serena Camp who is driving through our area. She has spotted a large group of hyenas converging near Maji

Fisi. We leave the den in hopes of witnessing a rare and exciting event.

As we approach, we spot two hyenas on the move, about sixty yards apart. Two more hyenas are ahead of them, but between the two pairs are two adult elephants, so we stay to the road. In the distance, we see six more hyenas. Ciara identifies them: it's Baez with a coterie of hyenas Nic and I haven't yet met: Rookie, Neon, Kesq, and others.

"What's happening?" asks Ciara. "Have we just caught the end of everything? Is this a border patrol?" Just like armies of warring nations, groups of hyenas regularly visit the borders of their territories, marking them with fresh scent saying, "Keep out: this land is ours!"

But now Ciara spots a group of seven other hyenas. We take off after the new group. They're about 270 yards southwest of Maji Fisi. About two hundred topi are facing them, compressed into a tight herd, alert and nervous. One of the hyenas—Wrath (she was in a litter named after deadly sins)—suddenly turns and breaks into a run. She's chasing not a topi, but a Grant's gazelle!

The gazelle, and a companion ahead of him, leap high, as if jumping over a series of invisible barriers—it's known as pronking or stotting. Gazelles do this for the benefit of the

Elephants block our path.

65

Wrath does a test run to determine if these gazelles might be easy to catch.

predator. They have two important messages to communicate: they've seen their would-be assailant; and they want to show off their own health and athleticism. This is information the hyena probably sought, Kay explains; a hyena often does a "test run" like this to see if a potential prey animal is worth pursuing—or just too fast and strong to try chasing.

Wrath gives up and rejoins the larger hunting party. The seven hyenas are flowing purposefully through the tall grass, heading south, only heads and sometimes the tops of their backs visible. They're clearly a coordi-nated, well-organized group. They're evenly spaced, like marching soldiers, spread out in a long line. Two of them raise black tails, bris-tling with excitement.

"They're excited—but about what? They sure look like they're going somewhere impor-tant," says Kay. Unfortunately, we can't leave the track, or we'll get stuck in the mud. But happily, the hyenas head toward our path: BUAR's in the lead, then Wrath, followed by Neon eight yards behind, and five others evenly spaced behind them. They stop, sniff, and mark the territory with paste. It's a border patrol!

Then the action inexplicably fizzles out. You never know what will happen—or what won't.

Kay and her researchers rely on glimpses like these—both ordinary days and relatively rare events—to reveal the true picture of hyena life. The hyenas' histories unfold much like our own. The stories of our lives, our com-munities, and our nations are told in a million ordinary days, as well as a relatively few quick, dramatic, life-changing events. And like the results of a human presidential election, the long-term effect of a hyena clan war might not be evident for years or even generations.

That's why long-term, detailed studies of animal communities, like Kay's hyenas, are so important. Her studies have transformed our understanding of Africa's most formidable, but often overlooked, predator.

True, hyenas are not all sweetness and light. They roll in vomit (to make themselves more interesting to other hyenas, explains Kay, like people use perfume and aftershave). They sometimes kill other hyenas' babies—Kay has personally seen ten cases of infanticide in her nearly thirty years of work. (She reminds us that killing infants is well known throughout human history, and continues in many human cultures today—notably in China and India, where baby boys are preferred, and girls may be killed at birth.)

Hyenas, Kay maintains, are fascinating because they are just so different: not only from the reputation that precedes them, but from most mammals in general. Because their clans are dominated by females, hyenas break the "rules" governing most mammalian societies—and that gives us a fresh way of looking at the more usual arrangement. And far from skulking, cowardly scavengers, spotted hyenas are among the most intelligent and social mammals on earth. "In their social intelligence, they're more like monkeys than anything else," says Kay.

This was a huge surprise to the research community. Kay's research cast this misunderstood mammal in an entirely new light. "We're proud of what we've been able to teach people about hyenas," says Kay. "But there's still so much to know."

A relaxed hyena shows off her formidable teeth.

SPOTTED HYENAS: FAST FACTS

A mother grooms her cub.

WHERE FOUND: Savannas, forests, hot deserts, and cold mountains, everywhere in Africa south of the Sahara, except the wettest parts of the Congo Basin.

RELATIVES: Two other species of hyena—striped and brown hyenas—and the small, slender, hole-digging aardwolf, which eats termites almost exclusively. All but the striped hyena live only in Africa. The striped hyena also ranges though Arabia and India into the Himalayas.

SIZE: Adults stretch about four feet long, may stand thirty inches at the shoulder, and may weigh more than one hundred thirty pounds. Females are usually 10 percent larger than males.

DIET: Just about anything. Large prey includes zebras, wildebeests, hartebeests, and other antelopes, supplemented with birds, lizards, snakes, insects, and carrion.

SPEED: Can run thirty miles an hour for two miles.

STRENGTH: A hyena's jaws are powerful enough to break open the leg bones of giraffes and hippopotamuses, bones that can be over three inches in diameter.

BREEDING: After four months of pregnancy, females give birth to up to three two-pound cubs. Babies nurse on extremely rich, high-protein milk for eight to twelve months. Kay's most successful matriarchs, alpha females Murphy and Bracket Shoulder, gave birth to eighteen and nineteen cubs respectively during their lifetimes, of which fourteen and thirteen survived to breeding age.

MATURITY: Young male hyenas leave their mothers around age two. Females stay with Mom, their young brothers, their sisters, aunts, and grandmothers for life. They start having cubs of their own at two to five years old.

PREDATORS: Lions, crocodiles, pythons, and humans.

LIFE EXPECTANCY: Only half of all cubs born survive to two years of age! Many are killed by lions. But a hyena who survives to adulthood might live more than twenty years in the wild, and up to forty in captivity.

Bibliography

BOOKS

Baynes-Rock, Marcus. *Among the Bone Eaters.* Philadelphia: Penn State University, 2015.

Estes, Richard Despard. *The Behavior Guide to African Mammals.* Berkeley, CA: University of California Press, 1991.

Kruuk, Hans. *The Spotted Hyena.* Chicago: University of Chicago Press, 1972.

Smith, J. E., and K. E. Holekamp. "Spotted Hyenas." In *Encyclopedia of Animal Behavior: Landmark Studies,* edited by M. Breed and J. Moore, 335–49. London: Elsevier, 2010.

Van Lawick-Goodall, Hugo and Jane. *Innocent Killers.* Boston: Houghton Mifflin, 1971.

WEB RESOURCES

Kay's research assistants and students blog from Masai Mara about their research: msuhyenas.blogspot.com

In 2011, Kay regularly contributed to "Scientist at Work," a blog for the *New York Times*: scientistatwork.blogs.nytimes.com/author/kay-e-holekamp

Listen to some of the awesome sounds a hyena makes: hyenatalk.weebly.com

Acknowledgments

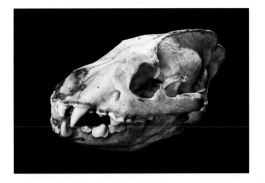

The flood that nearly forced an evacuation of Fisi Camp did nothing to dampen the incandescent delight of working with Kay Holekamp, her fabulous students, her wonderful staff, and the beautiful and fascinating hyenas. We hope our gratitude to them all is evident in these pages.

But there are also some people behind the scenes we want to thank.

We owe this book to Nora Lewin, a doctoral student of Kay's in November 2013, who first wrote to us suggesting the idea for it. We're also indebted to Hadley Courand, Kay's lab manager in 2016, who helped us organize our trip.

For reading and commenting on the manuscript, thank you, Joel Glick, Robert Matz, Robert and Judith Oksner, and Howard Mansfield. For the gorgeous design, thank you, Cara Llewellyn. For your thoughtful edits and support (not to mention enduring friendship), thank you, Kate O'Sullivan. For loaning the author her raingear (featured on page 36!) and other clothing, thank you, Jody Simpson. And thanks, as always, to *Agente Ultime,* Sarah Jane Freymann.

Index

Note: Page numbers in **bold** refer to photos and their captions.

SCIENTISTS IN THE FIELD

WHERE SCIENCE MEETS ADVENTURE

Check out these titles to meet more scientists who are out in the field—and contributing every day to our knowledge of the world around us.

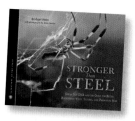

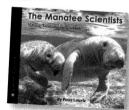

Looking for even more adventure? Craving updates on the work of your favorite scientists, as well as in-depth video footage, audio, photography, and more? Then visit the new Scientists in the Field website!

SCIENCEMEETSADVENTURE.COM